THE GREEKS

LOST CIVILIZATIONS

The books in this series explore the rise and fall of the great civilizations and peoples of the ancient world. Each book considers not only their history but their art, culture and lasting legacy and asks why they remain important and relevant in our world today.

Already published:

The Barbarians Peter Bogucki
Egypt Christina Riggs
The Etruscans Lucy Shipley
The Goths David M. Gwynn
The Greeks Philip Matyszak
The Indus Andrew Robinson
The Persians Geoffrey Parker and Brenda Parker

THE
GREEKS
LOST CIVILIZATIONS

PHILIP MATYSZAK

REAKTION BOOKS

For T. R. Eakle – the best of friends

Published by Reaktion Books Ltd
Unit 32, Waterside
44–48 Wharf Road
London N1 7UX, UK

www.reaktionbooks.co.uk

First published 2018, reprinted 2019
Copyright © Philip Matyszak 2018

Printed and bound in China by 1010 Printing International Ltd

A catalogue record for this book is available from the British Library

ISBN 978 1 78023 900 2

CONTENTS

CHRONOLOGY

Prehistory (all dates are approximate)

7200 BC	First evidence of human settlement in Greece appears with the discovery of Mesolithic burial sites in the Argolid (northeast Peloponnese)
7000–5500 BC	First evidence of villages, primitive trade and island settlements (that is, seafaring)
5000–3000 BC	Beginning of the 'palace culture' era. First fortified sites appear
3000 BC	The first bronze tools and weapons are used. The Bronze Age begins
3000–2000 BC	Beginning of the Minoan period in Crete
2000–1550 BC	The 'Middle Helladic Period' – an era of development in pottery, agriculture and the first established international trade routes
1700–1500 BC	Decline of Minoan culture, destruction of Cretan palaces. Rise of Mycenaean culture in mainland Greece. The Linear B system of writing is developed

1600–1200 BC	The so-called Heroic Age of the Mycenaean culture
1200 BC	The fall of Troy
1200–1000 BC	End of the Bronze Age civilization. The 'sea peoples' sack cities in the Levant, attack Egypt. Almost every major settlement in Greece is burned. Beginning of Greek colonial expansion

The Archaic era

c. 900 BC	Beginning of the Geometric period (so called after the distinctive vase patterns). Dorian cities such as Argos and Sparta become established
c. 800 BC	The Greeks develop a new alphabet modelled on Phoenician characters. The works of Homer and Hesiod are widely circulated. The Delphic oracle is established
776 BC	The dating of the Olympic Games begins
753 BC	Traditional date for the founding of Rome
733–690	Traditional date for the settlement by Corinth of Syracuse in Sicily. Other settlements founded in Italy and the western Mediterranean. Beginning of Magna Graecia
725 BC	The Lelantine War, the first war to involve almost all the major city-states of Greece
c. 685–560	Major era of settlement around the Black Sea

687 BC	The office of Archon – the major executive office in Athens – becomes elective
668 BC	Foundation of Byzantium by settlers from Megara
660 BC	Sparta conquers Messenia
c. 630 BC	Birth of Sappho in Lesbos. First Golden Age of Lyric poetry
621 BC	Draco introduces the first written law code in Greece. Punishments are so severe that the word 'Draconian punishments' passes into the language. The law codes are later rewritten by Solon
c. 571 BC	Birth of Pythagoras on the island of Samos

The Classical era

546 BC	Rise of the Persian empire. Persians reach the Mediterranean with the capture of Croesus of Lydia
c. 520 BC	Development of Athenian red-figure pottery
508 BC	Athens becomes a democratic state with the constitution of Kleisthenes
499 BC	Ionian cities backed by Athens rebel against Persia. Persian Wars begin
490 BC	Defeat of the Persians at Marathon

c. 484 BC	Aeschylus becomes the first of a succession of great Athenian playwrights
483 BC	Large silver deposits found at Larium near Athens. This bounty pays for later Athenian naval power
480 BC	Battle of Thermopylae, defeat of Leonidas and the 300
c. 480 BC	Failure of Carthaginian attempts to defeat Syracuse and master Sicily
479 BC	The battles of Mycale and Plataea remove the threat of Persian invasion of mainland Greece. The Persian Wars come to a standstill
477 BC	With Sparta no longer interested in fighting the Persians, Athens forms the Delian League and begins to subjugate its members into an Athens-based empire
461 BC	First Clash of Athens and Sparta in the Sacred War. This is the first of three wars generally called the Peloponnesian Wars
c. 460 BC	Pindar of Thebes writes his Lyric poems and panegyrics
c. 450–420 BC	Golden Age of Athenian theatre. Plays by Sophocles and Euripides
c. 440 BC	Herodotus writes his 'Inquiry' into the origins of the Persian Wars. This book, the *History*, is the first history book in the modern sense

c. 435 BC	The Statue of Zeus at Olympia is built and becomes one of the Seven Wonders of the world
431 BC	Sparta and allies declare war on Athens, starting the second Peloponnesian (Archidamian) War
c. 429 BC	Work begins on the Parthenon. Death of Pericles in the Athenian plague. Hippocrates of Cos writes his famous medical texts
424 BC	Exiled for failures as a commander in northern Greece, Thucydides starts work on his epic *History of the Peloponnesian War*
421 BC	Peace of Nicias ends the Archidamian War
415 BC	Athens fails disastrously in an attempt to conquer Sicily. Thousands of men are killed including three top Athenian generals
413 BC	The Peloponnesian Wars enter their final phase with the start of the Decelean (or Ionian) War
411 BC	Aristophanes produces the anti-war play *Lysistrata*, perhaps his most famous comedy
404 BC	Athens is finally defeated and surrenders to the Spartan commander Lysander
399 BC	Trial and death of Socrates
c. 384 BC	Plato founds his school at the Academy, which becomes a leading centre of philosophical thought. (The building had existed before, but was a gymnasium)

| 371 BC | Sparta defeated at Leuctra, beginning a period of Theban dominance |

The Hellenistic era

| 359 BC | Philip II becomes king of Macedonia |

| 356 BC | The temple of Artemis at Ephesus (one of the Seven Wonders of the ancient world) is burned. Alexander the Great is born |

| c. 340 BC | Aristotle of Stagira (northern Greece) is tutor to the young Alexander |

| 338 BC | Thebes is defeated by Philip II at Charonea. Thebes is destroyed and Philip forms the Hellenic League (the League of Corinth) with the intent of uniting Greece against Persia |

| 336 BC | Philip II is assassinated. Alexander becomes king |

| c. 335 BC | Aristotle founds the Lyceum in Athens |

| 334–333 BC | Alexander invades the Persian empire, winning victories at Granicus and Issus |

| 331 BC | Conquest of Egypt by Macedon, foundation of Alexandria. The Persians suffer their final defeat at Gaugamela |

| c. 326 BC | Greek armies campaign in Sogdiana and India |

| 323 BC | Death of Alexander |

323–311 BC	Successor wars, ending with the partition of Alexander's empire between his surviving generals
c. 320–311 BC	Menander becomes the leading exponent of Athenian New Comedy
310–307 BC	Foundation of the Stoic and Epicurean schools of philosophy, both in Athens
301 BC	The Battle of Issus divides the Hellenic world into Macedonian, Seleucid and Ptolemaic spheres of influence
c. 300 BC	Euclid publishes his *Elements of Geometry*, which is to become a standard school text for the next 2,000 years
289 BC	The Greek god of medicine, Asclepius, is rehoused in a new temple in Rome
c. 283 BC	The Great Library of Alexandria opens its doors
280–275 BC	Pyrrhus of Epirus attempts to conquer Italy and is held back by Rome. The Roman Republic goes on to absorb the Greek cities of southern Italy
c. 280 BC	Another of the Seven Wonders, the Colossus, is constructed at the harbour of Rhodes
274–271 BC	The first Syrian War between Egypt and the Seleucids
c. 270 BC	Aristarchus of Samos speculates that the Earth revolves around the sun

260–200 BC	The second to fifth Syrian Wars. These wars between Egypt and Seleucia ultimately achieved little, but debilitated the Seleucid kingdom and helped its ultimate collapse
c. 250 BC	Eratosthenes calculates the circumference of the Earth (and gets it very nearly right)
247 BC	Arsaces I establishes the Parthian dynasty and takes Parthia out of Seleucid control. The last of the ancient world's Seven Wonders – the Great Lighthouse – is built in Alexandria
212 BC	Death of Archimedes, fall of Syracuse, the last great Greek city in the west
c. 200 BC	Bactria slips from Seleucid control. A series of Indo-Greek kingdoms rise and fall in its place
200–196 BC	Rome invades Greece and defeats Philip V of Macedonia at Cynoscephalae. Greece is declared 'free'
190 BC	The Battle of Magnesia sees Rome defeat Antiochus III of Seleucia. Asia Minor falls from Seleucid control
172–168 BC	Rome conquers Macedon in the Third Macedonian War. Macedon becomes the first Hellenistic kingdom absorbed by Rome
168 BC	Start of the rebellion of the Maccabees in Judaea
161 BC	Greek philosophers expelled from Rome for 'corrupting Roman morality'

c. 150 BC	The complex Antikythera mechanism is built to compute the movements of the sun and moon
146 BC	Rome sacks Corinth and makes Greece a province
c. 141 BC	Parthia takes control of Persis and the Silk Road
c. 140 BC	Rise of the Philhellenic movement in Rome
c. 128 BC	Alexander of Antioch carves the Venus de Milo
102–84 BC	Seleucia devastated by civil wars
87–86 BC	Siege and sack of Athens by the Romans
83 BC	Tigranes of Armenia becomes 'protector' of the remnants of the Seleucid empire
63 BC	Pompey dissolves the remnants of the Seleucid kingdom and establishes the province of Syria
30 BC	Death of Cleopatra. Egypt becomes a Roman possession

Greece and Rome

19 BC	Virgil completes the *Aeneid*, an epic poem uniting the Greek and Roman origin myths
AD 55	Birth of Epictetus of Hierapolis in the reign of Nero, Epictetus becomes Rome's leading Stoic philosopher

AD 67	The Philhellene emperor Nero competes in the Olympic Games
c. AD 70	The Gospel of Mark is written (probably in Greek, though this is controversial). The Gospels of Matthew and Luke follow in the next two decades
AD 97	Plutarch of Charonea publishes his *Parallel Lives*, linking the biographies of great figures in the past of Greece and Rome
AD 124	Hadrian completes the temple of Zeus in Athens, 640 years after the building project was begun
c. AD 150–70	Lucian of Samosata produces a series of witty and satirical compositions
AD 330	Foundation of Constantinople on the site of Byzantium
AD 391	The Serapeum – the core of the Library of Alexandria – is destroyed for being a pagan temple
AD 393	The last Olympic Games before they are abolished as a pagan festival
AD 395	The Roman empire permanently splits into a Greek east and Latin west
AD 476	The Byzantine empire becomes the heir to the legacy of Greece and Rome

AD 526	Justinian becomes emperor. His attempts to reconquer the west succeed in briefly regaining Rome, but plague and famine weaken his empire and the reconquest is abandoned
AD 529	Production of the *Codex Justinianus*, a comprehensive compilation of Roman law that became the basis of most modern European legal systems
AD 532	Building of the Hagia Sophia, the greatest Greek religious building since the Parthenon
c. AD 610	The empire abandons Latin as an official language and reverts entirely to Greek
AD 612–90	Muslim expansion takes Syria, Palestine, Egypt and north Africa from Byzantine control
AD 717	Muslim siege of Constantinople is beaten back
c. AD 1050	The Normans conquer Byzantine possessions in Italy
AD 1071	Defeat at Manzikert loses most of Asia Minor to the Turks
AD 1204	Crusaders attack and sack Constantinople
AD 1453	The Ottomans capture Constantinople and destroy the Byzantine empire

Early Greek civilization drew heavily upon the older and more established civilization of the Egyptians.

PROLOGUE

The Greek world of antiquity extended in time and space far beyond what we today call 'Greece'. Many modern tourists who are surprised to find the ruins of Greek cities in Turkey might be even more surprised to know that many Greek cities of equal antiquity are still thriving today with names such as Naples ('Nea polis' or 'New City') in Italy and Marseille (Massalia) in France. It is even more remarkable that Ai-Khanoum in northern Afghanistan (Alexandria on the Oxus) was founded by the Greek ruler Seleucus I in around 275 BC, and is one of dozens of formerly Greek cities scattered around central Asia.

At its peak, Greek civilization extended for over a thousand kilometres east and west from the Greek mainland. Syria, Egypt and Babylonia were once Hellenistic kingdoms. Furthermore, many of those famous Greeks of whom students learn in high school seldom if ever spent time in Greece itself. These include Herodotus, Sappho, Euclid, Pythagoras and Archimedes.

There are many books covering the history of Classical Greece, though that era represents only a minor portion of the overall history of the Greeks of antiquity. Much of the rest has been forgotten, or is mentioned only when the Greeks of other times and places came into contact with different cultures. This book takes the opposite approach. The Greek mainland is seldom mentioned and the focus is on the Greeks elsewhere in the ancient world, especially in what today we would call the Middle East and Central Asia, places that many ancient Greeks simply called 'home'.

Greek theatres showed the same plays and had the same architectural features, whether they were intimate venues in Spain (top) or seated thousands, as did this theatre at Delphi in Greece (bottom).

This book is the story of the Greeks outside Greece. It covers a period of over 2,000 years, from prehistoric Greek settlements on the shores of the Black Sea to the fall of the last great Greek city of the medieval world – mighty Constantinople. Between these two points we see the rise of Greek power in the Aegean Sea, the

Shallow drinking cup featuring Dionysiac revels, of a type typical in early Classical Athens.

conquests of Alexander and the sprawling Hellenistic successor kingdoms that ruled an area as large as the later Roman empire. This book will go on to argue that Greek culture in Asia Minor and the Middle East was largely unchanged by the Roman conquest, and reverted almost entirely to its Greek roots as the long-lived Byzantine empire thereafter.

It is worth noting that all the Seven Wonders of the ancient world – the Great Pyramid at Giza, the Lighthouse at Alexandria, the Hanging Gardens of Babylon, the Colossus of Rhodes, the Temple of Artemis, the Statue of Zeus at Olympia and the Mausoleum at Halicarnassus – were either built by Greeks or in lands later ruled by Greeks. Yet only one – the Statue of Zeus – was actually in mainland Greece itself.

The world of greater Greece was an astonishing place that combined huge intellectual energy, a remarkable humanism and a wonderful sense of aesthetics. With a cast of characters ranging from decadent despots and eccentric geniuses to artists of sublime ability, the people of the extended Greek world have had a huge effect on the development of Western civilization. This book will show that, unbeknownst to us, their presence is still everywhere around us today.

This is their story.

Greek and later Hellenistic sculpture combined aesthetics and realism in a manner unsurpassed even today.

ONE
THE GREEKS BEFORE ALEXANDER

In 1200 BC ancient Greece was part of a developing and integrated civilization that stretched from India to the western Mediterranean. This was the peak of the Bronze Age, when trade routes reached from Britain deep into Asia, and an Egyptian pharaoh might be entombed along with vases from Mesopotamia, olive oil from Cyprus, cedar from the Lebanon and bronze artefacts made with tin from Welsh mines. This was the age of the Hittites, the bull-leaping Minoans of Crete and the palace civilization of Mycenaean Greece, a world later remembered in the legends of Hercules and Helen of Troy. It was advanced, sophisticated, prosperous – and doomed.

When disaster struck, the magnitude was as vast as the cause is incomprehensible. In the fifty years between 1050 and 1000 BC almost every city of note in the ancient world was sacked and destroyed. Even mighty Egypt, protected by her natural barriers of sea and desert, came under major assault by the *Hyskos*, the Sea People, and under that attack the state almost collapsed into anarchy. Lacking the natural defences of Egypt, the Hittite and Minoan civilizations were wiped out. Trade collapsed, populations went into catastrophic decline and civilization in the western Mediterranean fell into a 'Dark Age' that lasted for over 250 years.

What caused the collapse has been the cause of much academic debate in the modern era. Volcanic eruptions have been suggested, especially the vast explosion of the volcano at Thera (modern Santorini), and the climate changes brought about by such eruptions. Thera threw an estimated 60 cubic kilometres of debris into

Archaic era vase showing one of the 'black ships' described by Homer in the *Iliad*, book II, 'The Catalogue of Ships', ll. 484–580.

the atmosphere, causing severe weather effects that were recorded in contemporary ancient China. Barbarian invasions, severe plagues and systemic economic collapse have also been suggested triggers for the Dark Age, and even if these disasters did not cause the collapse, they certainly contributed to it.

Greece was not spared, nor was its Mycenaean civilization. Every ancient city unearthed by archaeologists in Greece reveals a destruction layer dated to this period. Whatever happened to these cities in the last decades of the eleventh century BC included burning, looting and corpses left unburied in the streets. The survivors of the catastrophe huddled in isolated valleys and hilltop forts. Over the following decades the art of writing was lost, and trade became a matter of barter between local villages.

The population of Greece also changed. In later Greek tradition a people known as the Dorians, who called themselves 'the sons of Hercules', swept south from the Balkans and occupied most of the Peloponnese. Thereafter the Greeks identified themselves as either the original Ionian and Arcadian peoples or the invading Dorians (the Spartans in particular identified with the latter group).

The Dorian invasion displaced the original inhabitants of the Peloponnese, who fled abroad, laying the foundation of the Greek empire in the centuries to come. Or so the ancient Greeks believed. Modern research has shown that the picture was considerably more

'I see men bearing shields and spears, together with horses and curve-fronted chariots.' The playwright Aeschylus (525–456 BC) describes a scene such as that depicted on this vase in his play *The Supplicants*.

Limestone statue of Hercules from Archaic-era Cyprus. Egyptian influence can be seen in the stance of and the kilt worn by the figure.

complex than that. For a start, it is uncertain whether the Dorians replaced the population of the Peloponnese, assimilated with it or were the original population to begin with. Nor were the Dorians alone the cause of the collapse of the Mycenaean civilization. However, in this study we are less concerned with causes than with results, and the result of the Dark Age collapse was to spread Greek civilization around the Mediterranean and beyond.

When the mists of the Dark Age began to clear into the world of Archaic Greece, not only were there Greeks living far beyond Greece, but these 'foreign' cities were among the torch-bearers leading Greek culture and thought into the new era. To the ancients, 'Greece' included parts of Asia Minor, the islands of the Aegean Sea, Sicily and much of southern Italy. The main divisions of the Greek world were 'Hellas', comprising Greece itself, Ionia, which was the Greek cities of the Aegean Islands and those on the coast of Asia Minor, and Magna Graecia, which included Sicily and South Italy. In total there were hundreds of such colonies (the city of Miletus alone established thirty). From Mainace in southern Iberia to Phasis on the Black Sea coast of modern Georgia, Greek colonies were woven along the coastline like 'a Greek fringe on a barbarian cloak' (as Cicero put it in *De republica*, 2.9).

As well as sharing in a unified Greek culture, these cities had much else in common. For a start, almost all were on or near the coast. As the philosopher Plato famously remarked, the Greek cities sat around the Mediterranean 'like frogs around a pond' (*Phaedo*, 109b). From Halicarnassus in Asia Minor to Syracuse in Sicily, the pattern of colonization seems to have been for the Greeks to find and fortify an island base just off the coast. Then, once trade and familiarity had softened up the locals, the Greeks moved to the mainland opposite and set up their colony, with the island serving as a fortress of last refuge.

As an example of how important this settlement technique was to the early colonists, the city of Chalcedon came to be known to later Greeks as 'the City of the Blind'. This was because the founding fathers apparently missed the obvious attractions of the site that later became Constantinople just over the Bosporus strait. However, Chalcedon had the Kadikoy Peninsula, which served as the 'offshore base', and this was lacking on the prospective settlement site on the European side.

Most cities retained a sentimental attachment to their founding city (Chalcedon was founded by Greeks from Megara). These links, as well as the more material links of trade and commerce, brought prosperity to the new colonies as goods from their diverse hinterlands were swapped around by fleets of traders who plied the seas. The Athenians exported vases to Phoenicia in return for that land's famed purple dye, while the Phoenicians often re-exported the vases to Egypt in exchange for grain and papyrus. Chinese silk and Persian slippers imported by the cities of Anatolia might be exchanged in Rhegium for Italian wax, cheese and slaves. Between feuding with the Sicilian Greeks, the Carthaginians traded ivory for Cypriot tin or Etrurian bronzes.

Through trade, cities such as Corinth prospered. In fact Corinth benefited so greatly from its position on the narrowest part of the Peloponnesian isthmus that the city was often called 'wealthy Corinth', just as the lifestyle of Sybaris in Italy was so luxurious that even today the word 'sybaritic' describes self-indulgent decadence.

With the movement of goods from the diverse hinterlands of the Greek world came exposure to different cultures, ideas, religions and philosophies. The stimulus that resulted from this exchange brought about the fifth-century intellectual revolution, and the thought processes that have shaped our modern world.

Empires of the mind

When we look at the explosion of intellectual energy in early Classical Greece, we can see that much of what the Greeks developed was not original. There are clear traces of Semitic (Phoenician and Jewish) influence, and the Greeks also built on the earlier work of the Babylonians. The controversial 'Black Athena' hypothesis has alleged that much of Greek philosophy was adopted from African thought and imported via Egypt. While this idea has come under academic attack, it is at least increasingly probable that the Greek alphabet was developed in Egypt from Semitic roots. Linguists note that the word 'alphabet' itself comes from the Semitic words

Greek myths reflect the international fusion that created later Greek culture. Here we see Titian's portrayal of Dionysus (a god with origins in Asia Minor) meeting Ariadne of Crete on the island of Naxos.

aelph (bull) and *beth* (house). ('Beth lehem' literally means 'house of bread'.)

However, while earlier forms of writing such as Egyptian hiero-glyphics relied on pictographs, the Greeks went further by using symbols to reproduce the sounds of their spoken language. Where the Egyptians used a picture to show (for example) a cat, Greek used symbols to represent the sounds of the spoken word for 'cat'. The example of the alphabet shows that the Greeks did not blindly adopt foreign ideas; they analysed, adapted and improved them by incorporating ideas and concepts from the many other cultures with which they were in contact. The result was a synthesis (*synthesis* being a Greek word and concept) that was uniquely Greek.

Likewise, we can trace the arrival of the Classical Greek gods from their origin stories. Zeus came from Crete, Aphrodite from

Marble grave marker from Archaic Athens. The inscription on the base reads 'To dear Me[gakles], on his death, his father with his dear mother set [me] up as a monument.'

Cyprus, Dionysus and the witch-goddess Hecate from Anatolia. The earliest legends of Hercules come not from Greece, but from Egypt. However, once adopted by the Greeks, these gods changed in fundamental ways that adapted them to the Greek view of religion.

In Greek mythology the Olympian gods came to rule the world after overthrowing the previous generation of gods in a literally titanic battle (both Zeus and his predecessors were of a gigantic race known as the Titans). This battle may reflect the struggle by which the new pantheon of gods imported from abroad replaced their native predecessors in the minds of worshippers.

With the replacement of the gods came new ways of thinking about religion. In previous belief systems, the world operated in the way it did through the direct agency of the gods. The corn, for example, grew because the goddess Demeter willed it. And that was that, because the workings of the gods were basically unknowable. However, Greek thought in the Archaic and Classical eras came to see the gods as forces. Zeus was the force of order, Aphrodite represented the power of love and Demeter the impulse that caused the fields to be fruitful, and so on. Once the world was seen as being run by a pattern of interlocking forces it became possible to view the cosmos as a machine. It helped that the Greeks had no religious dogma – defining dogma as religious beliefs that the clergy regard as indisputable and unchallengeable – and no concept of heresy. The Greeks were wary of blasphemy and sacrilege, but only because they believed that their gods cared little about collateral damage while they were avenging personal affronts.

Therefore, if it did not interfere with the community's worship of the gods, the average Greek was free to believe what he liked. Once Greek philosophers came to believe that the world was a machine, it was natural for them to take up the challenge of fig-uring out how that machine worked, and Greek religious thought had no ideological objection to such a line of enquiry.

From there the Greeks developed the concept of empiricism – the process of observing through personal experience and then rationalizing the knowledge gained through that experience. This is the basis of the modern scientific process. While the concept seems obvious to the modern mind, in the ancient world this represented a huge intellectual breakthrough that led directly to the modern disciplines of biology, mathematics, physics and chemistry.

While modern philosophy is mostly concerned with the self, its ethics and morality, the first 'lovers of wisdom' (which is what 'philosophers' actually means) gave themselves a far broader scope, addressing questions that were once left for priests to answer. 'Where do things come from?' 'What are they made from?' 'Can nature be described by processes?'

Some of the answers were wildly wrong. Greek astronomers understood that the Earth was round by observing its shadow on the moon during eclipses, and from there they quickly realized that the moon circled the Earth. They then jumped to the erroneous conclusion that the rest of the universe circled the Earth as well, and drew up an elaborate – and totally false – cosmology that nevertheless explained all observed phenomena. This included some stars that moved about the constellations when all others were fixed. These stars were the planets, from the Greek *planetes* or 'wanderers'.

Greek thought thus removed the superstition surrounding events such as eclipses, which became understood and predictable. For example, the Greek statesman Pericles once explained matters to a sailor by holding his cloak between the sailor and the sun and patiently explaining that eclipses were just like that, but bigger and further away.

On Gaia – the Earth – the first table of the elements included only earth, air, water and fire, since the early Greeks reckoned that everything was made of a greater or lesser amount of these. In the fifth century the philosophers Democritus and Leucippus concluded that all matter had a single building block. This could be found by cutting something into halves until the final remaining part was that basic uncuttable unit. This was called 'the uncuttable' or in Greek, *atomus*. Leucippus argued that the material world was made from these 'atoms' arranged in almost infinite combinations to make up the objects with which we interact every day.

The investigative process described here went on through the next five hundred years with steady advances in all the sciences.

By the end of the Hellenistic era, philosophy had established with remarkable accuracy things like the size of the Earth and the distance to the moon. The basics of how to move objects with levers were mathematically established ('Give me somewhere to stand and I could move the Earth,' muttered Archimedes), as were the principles of geometry and how to build a working steam engine (the aeolipile).

It was an era of progress and creativity that slowed only with the coming of the Roman empire, and which ground virtually to a halt when that empire fell. When the Renaissance and the later Enlightenment began the building of modern Europe, the great thinkers of those eras pretty much bypassed the philosophical and religious shibboleths of the previous thousand years and carried on where the Greek philosophers had left off.

Greeks outside Greece

One of the interesting things about early Greek philosophy is that most of it happened away from the Greek mainland. The first philosophers came from Miletus, a city off the coast of Anatolia at the mouth of the winding river whose name has given the world the word 'meander'. A bit later, philosophers from the nearby island of Samos concluded that the universe was mathematically coherent (two plus two always equalled four), and it behoved humanity to bring their lives into the same harmonious balance. The Ephesian school of philosophy, as its name suggests, originated in the city of Ephesus, which was actually on the mainland coast of Asia Minor.

The other major branch of Greek philosophy was also not in Greece, but in southern Italy. The Elean school (Elea is modern Velia, in the province of Salerno) produced Zeno and his famous paradoxes and the principle of *reductio ad absurdum*, which argued that accepting a false principle or refuting a true one eventually leads to untenable conclusions. Other Western philosophers were based in Agrigentum in Sicily (the Pluralists) and Croton, a city on the southwestern Italian coast.

Several of the later pre-Socratics (as these early philosophers were called) came from Thrace, the wild lands around the Black

Sea which the Greeks had also settled just after the Dark Age. These included the Sophists (who believed that reality was subjective, which is why any modern argument based on this premise is called 'sophistry') and Leucippus the Atomist, referred to above.

Perhaps the most well-known of these philosophers was and still is Pythagoras, whose rule 'the square of the hypotenuse is equal to the squares of the other two sides' is still laboriously recited by schoolchildren today. One of the interesting things about Pythagoras was that he only briefly visited mainland Greece, spending most of his life in Ionia, especially Samos, and later moving to southern Italy.

It is not only philosophers who contributed much to mainstream Greek culture without spending much time in mainland Greece. There is the legendary Homer, whose verses did much to shape classical thought and approaches to religion. Even today, when we 'mentor' or 'hector' someone we are re-enacting the roles of those characters in Homer's *Iliad*, and the Trojan horse and Achilles' heel are almost as much a part of modern culture as they were of Greek culture.

The origin of Homer is disputed, and some modern scholars question whether 'Homer' was actually a single individual. Nevertheless, few ancient sources base the writer of the *Iliad* and the *Odyssey* in mainland Greece. In fact, the most authoritative source – though not now believed to have been written by Homer himself – is the Homeric 'Hymn to Apollo', which includes the verse:

> Should some stranger ask, 'Maidens, which singer who comes here brings you the most delight?' you must all answer together in your gentle voices, 'Blind is the poet, and he comes from the rock-bound isle of Chios.' (3, ll. 165–70)

If Homer came from Chios, another poet came from nearby Lesbos – a woman whose homoerotic poetry has come to define those with her sexual orientation as 'lesbian'. This was Sappho, one of the greatest lyric poets of the ancient world. ('Lyric' poems were meant to be sung to the accompaniment of a lyre.) Rather like Pythagoras, Sappho started in Ionia and finished in southern

Italy. It is uncertain if she ever spent time in mainland Greece along the way.

Another concept that the Greeks developed further than anyone had before was the idea of 'inquiry' into events, the analysis of what had happened in the past and a search for the root causes of major developments. The Greek word for such inquiry was 'Historia'. There had been 'histories' written before, but these were simple

Statuette of a doll from the Spartan colony of Tarentum in Italy, from the 3rd century BC. The female figurine is nude but wears an elaborate headdress.

This terracotta of Bellepheron slaying the Chimera in Asia Minor is a reminder that the Greeks had centuries-long contact with the region, and that to them the Persians were the invading interlopers.

annalistic chronicles without any analysis of why things happened as they did, other than when this is given as the will of a particular deity.

It fell to a Greek from outside Greece to write the first history in which the influence of the gods played little part. This was the inquiry by Herodotus of Halicarnassus into the causes of the Persian war with the Greeks. It is largely thanks to Herodotus that we know the details of the battles of Marathon, Thermopylae and Salamis, battles where the Persian invasion of the Greek mainland was checked and ultimately thrown back. It is less well known that, technically speaking, Herodotus was on the losing side. That is, as a citizen of Halicarnassus in Asia Minor, he was a subject of the Persian empire. Indeed, Artemisia, the Queen of Halicarnassus, won high praise from the Persian King of Kings for her conduct in the battle of Salamis in 480 BC.

Herodotus is justly known as 'the father of history' for his account of the Persian Wars. However, his *History* is also part travelogue and part rambling collection of anecdotes from the many lands through which he passed. Because his city was a part of the Persian empire, Herodotus was able to travel widely through the Middle East, and his is the earliest Western account of India. He probably visited Egypt and this visit yielded a wealth of anecdotes, including the tale of a Greek who crossed the Sahara to the banks of the River Niger (which Herodotus mistakenly thought was the Nile taking a sharp westward bend).

Herodotus also gave an account of the circumnavigation of Africa by a Phoenician captain, remarking dubiously, 'These men made a statement which I do not myself believe . . . that as they sailed on a westerly course round the southern end of Africa, they had the sun on their right – to the north of them.' (Herodotus, *History*, 4.42). This is, however, exactly where the sun would have been, as any inhabitant of modern Cape Town can confirm.

Finally, an honourable mention must be made of a much later Greek, the inventor and mathematician Archimedes. Famous for the 'eureka' ('I've got it!') moment that propelled him from his bathtub, Archimedes visited Egypt but spent most of his life in his native Sicily. He is never recorded as setting foot on the Greek mainland. He lived many years after the others described here, being killed after the Roman capture of Syracuse in 212 BC, but his life was proof that the Greek genius for invention lasted throughout this era, and that Archimedes, like many others, is regarded as quintessentially Greek despite having little connection to the Greek mainland itself.

Most forms of Greek civilization flourished outside mainland Greece. The exception was playwriting, and here Athens was supreme. No city elsewhere could rival the plays – still performed today – of Sophocles, Aeschylus, Euripides, Menander, Aristophanes and their contemporaries.

In fact, the defeat of the Persian empire's attempt to assimilate mainland Greece was followed by a golden age of Greek culture. The name of this era comes from the Athenian leader of the time, Pericles. Though Pericles was the acknowledged leader of Athens, he had no official status. At this time Athens was experimenting with an extreme form of democracy in which the only state officials had administrative roles in preparing the agenda for the people's

Names like Philippos and Hippocrates show the importance of horses in early Greek society, as does this Archaic era picture of a horse on a Greek vase.

assembly, and even these officials were either elected or chosen by lot. As a result, in theory a shoemaker had as much right to address the assembly as did Pericles. (Despite this democratic ideal, in reality, the respect still afforded to the rich and aristocratic meant that the leaders of Athens tended to be people like Pericles, who was both.)

The democratic idea of how a state should be governed had numerous detractors around Greece, and even more in later autocratic eras. The suspicion of this form of government and the critical opinion of later historians is now embodied in the word 'democracy', which can be construed as having a derogatory meaning along the lines of 'mob rule'. The root word *kratos* describes acts of force or violence, and it is significant that this was used rather than a kinder description such as *demarchy*, meaning 'rule by the people'.

The Athenians did not invent democracy – indeed, a crude form of it existed in Archaic Sparta – but the Athenians went further than almost anyone in handing power to the people as a whole. (The 'people' being male, adult citizens of Athens in good standing. Only satirical playwrights such as the subversive Aristophanes would suggest something as silly as assemblywomen.)

Nevertheless, much has been made of Athenian democracy, even though it was not the root of modern European-style democracies, which developed from Anglo-Saxon tribal meetings called 'moots'. Furthermore, unfettered democracy was practised only in a minority of Greek cities for a relatively brief period. During the later Hellenistic era, democracy was permitted only as an option for some local governments, but under overall monarchical control. Nevertheless, Greek democracy is rightly praised, not least because it went on to influence the government of the Roman Republic, which practised its own (restricted) form of democracy. The Roman version of democracy in turn influenced the Founding Fathers of the United States, which is why that country has (for example) a Senate.

The Peloponnesian War and the rise of Macedon

Once, there was a dark side to the Athenian Golden Age. Basically, it was built upon betrayal. The Greeks had banded together under Spartan leadership to resist the Persian invasion. However, once the immediate threat of Persian conquest had been overcome, the introverted Spartans relinquished the leadership of the Greeks, and this leadership was taken up by Athens. Under Athens the contributions of men and ships by various independent city-states to the common defence of Greece tended to become a cash payment to the Athenians, who undertook to supply the men and ships for the others.

Gradually this payment became tribute, rising every year, with collection enforced by Athenian arms. Those states which had assumed that they were Athenian allies had become Athenian subjects, and money originally intended to raise armies to fight the Persians was diverted to the glorification of Athens. Peoples who had freely joined the league to defend themselves against the Persians now found themselves reluctantly paying for building projects in Athens. The Athenians unashamedly called the states under their control 'the Athenian empire'.

The rise of Athens caused unease in Sparta, and the restless and expansionist Athenian character caused Sparta's allies to urge that something be done about the ever-growing power that other Greeks saw less as inspiring than as a direct threat. The war between the Athenian empire and the Peloponnesian League led by Sparta lasted almost thirty years and took in almost the entire Greek world, from Thrace to Sicily. In the end Athens was defeated, her navy exhausted and the economy ruined. The contemporary historian Thucydides, who wrote the definitive history of the conflict, reported that Sparta had been sustained through the latter part of the conflict by Persia, which had subsidized the Spartan war effort with massive transfers of bullion that had sustained the fleets that eventually broke Athenian sea power.

Post-war Athens soon shook off a Spartan-imposed oligarchy, but the city never regained its pre-war exuberance. Even before this war Persia had developed a great respect for the military prowess of the Greek hoplites who had beaten them on so many occasions. The return of peace meant that the Greeks were available to work as Persian mercenaries and many of them did so, serving Persian masters in areas as diverse as Thrace and Egypt. Perhaps the most famous group of Greek mercenaries were the 10,000 who were hired to help a pretender called Cyrus in his attempt to take the Persian throne from his brother.

In the climactic battle at Cunaxa in 401 BC, the Greeks easily vanquished their opponents. However, Cyrus was killed in the struggle and his rebellion collapsed, leaving the 10,000 Greeks stranded in hostile country just north of Babylon in modern Iraq. The story of how the 10,000 fought their way back to the coast of the Black Sea and thence to Greece is one of the epics of military history, preserved today as 'The March of the Ten Thousand' written by Xenophon, one of the army's leaders. The subtext of this description was the superiority of Greek armies against their numerically superior Persian enemies, and nowhere was this text studied more closely than in Macedon.

Until the middle of the fourth century BC the more southerly Greeks had always been sceptical as to whether the huge semi-feudal kingdom to the north was properly Greek at all. Certainly the state was useful as a bulwark against invading northern barbarians. However, the southern Greek people had largely abandoned kings and regarded the *polis* city-state as the standard unit of government. The dialect, customs and government of Macedon seemed foreign to them, though they grudgingly allowed Macedonian kings to participate in pan-Hellenic Games such as the Olympics (to which people such as the Syracusans were welcomed without hesitation).

This changed when Philip II became king of Macedon in 359 BC. Philip had spent his youth as a hostage in Thebes, at a time when that state was perhaps the dominant city in Greece. He proved a keen student of Theban military affairs, and when he returned to Macedon as king he rapidly applied his knowledge to the Macedonian army. His creation, the Macedonian pike phalanx, became the primary instrument of Greek military power for the next two centuries until it was finally broken by the Roman legions. Following the contemporary Greek trend, Philip equipped his phalangites with a type of long spear called the *sarissa*. The length of the spears meant that soldiers in the second or third line of a phalanx could contribute directly to a battle, confronting the enemy with a wall of spears that was practically impossible to defeat in head-on combat.

When Philip came to power, Macedon was in some disarray. Philip faced rivals for his throne within the kingdom and threats from powerful barbarian confederations outside. (In fact, Philip originally took power as regent for his dead brother's young son, but he quickly allocated the throne to himself.) Using a mixture of military force and persuasion Philip drove back the barbarian invaders and turned his attention to northern Greece. By conquering the lands around the cities of Amphipolis and Crenides (the latter city he renamed Philippi), he came into possession of the rich mines that were to fund his later bouts of conquest.

By 354 BC Philip was master of Thessaly, and incidentally had absorbed the Greek cities along the Balkan coast into his kingdom. Before then he had lost an eye (from a wound at the siege of Methone in northern Greece) and gained a son, whom he gave the traditional family name of Alexander. Philip continued to intervene in affairs in central Greece, and asserted the authority of Macedonian arms by crushing an alliance led by the Athenians and Thebans at the Battle of Charonea in 338 BC.

This battle made Philip hegemon of Greece, its ruler in all but name. Only the Peloponnesians, led by Sparta, defied him. To the Spartans Philip sent a warning – 'If I bring my army I will pillage your land, slay your people and destroy your city.' The Spartan reply was a typically laconic 'If.' In the end Philip left Sparta alone.

Philip seems not to have seen himself as the king of Greece. Rather he imagined himself as the man who would lead the united Greek peoples to victory over the real enemy – the Persian empire. Therefore his activities after the victory at Charonea were those not of a conqueror but of a diplomat. In 337 he called for a conference near Corinth, at which he urged the Greek states to put aside their differences and aid him in defeating the Persian foe once and for all. The congress ended with the formation of the League of Corinth, at which, with the exception of Sparta, all the Greek states agreed to become allies. (Philip maintained that Macedon was one of these 'Greek states', and the other Greeks were by now in no position to disagree.) Macedon agreed not to attack League members, or to interfere with their internal politics, but Philip also left 'peace-keeping' garrisons at strategic locations about Greece in case any of his new friends had second thoughts.

The following year Philip returned to Macedon to prepare his army for the invasion of the Persian empire. In October of that year he was at Aegae, the ancient capital of the kingdom. At the time he was celebrating the diplomatic marriage of his daughter to the king of Epirus. In order to make himself more approachable

The 'Corinthian' style of helmet, used by the Greeks for centuries, was being phased out in Alexander's time in favour of more open helmets that allowed members of a phalanx to see and hear signals more easily.

to the Greek ambassadors who had gathered for the occasion, Philip was only lightly guarded. For reasons no one has been able to establish with any certainty, one of his bodyguards took the opportunity to kill his king. In later ages suspicion fell upon Philip's wife, Olympias. It was suspected that she had engineered the assassination in order to ensure that her son Alexander succeeded to the Macedonian throne. Alexander and Philip had a turbulent relationship, and though Alexander was currently in favour and the designated heir, no one could tell how long that would last.

Thus Alexander came to the Macedonian throne in 336 BC, to embark on a thirteen-year career of conquest that would expand Greek power and influence further than anyone could have imagined.

TWO

ALEXANDER
AND THE EAST

W hile the career of Alexander the Great appears at first glance to be an unbroken string of victories, it is worth noting that it almost did not get off the ground at all. For a start, once Philip II had been assassinated there was no guarantee that Alexander would be accepted as his successor. True, Philip had been grooming his son for that role, and Alexander had some military experience gained both in fighting off barbarian raids and in commanding an elite unit at the Battle of Charonea. He also had some experience of government, as Philip had left him in charge of Macedon while he was campaigning in Greece.

But Alexander was only twenty years old when his father died, and some of Philip's older and more experienced generals were dubious about putting themselves under the command of a younger and relatively inexperienced commander. Furthermore, Alexander's mother, Olympias, was a non-Macedonian, and currently a disgraced exile, so some felt that Amyntas – the young king whom Philip had supplanted – should now be restored to his throne.

Fortunately a senior general called Antipater supported Alexander (as he would throughout Alexander's life). At Antipater's urging, the army threw its support behind the young heir, who consequently came to the throne as Alexander III of Macedon. To his friends and supporters, Alexander was usually generous and open-hearted, but he was viciously brutal to those whom he saw as a threat. Amyntas was swiftly executed. Likewise, once Olympias was restored from exile, Philip II's former queen – a woman called Cleopatra – was savagely murdered along with most of her family.

Philip II of Macedon, who laid the foundations for the empire established by his son Alexander the Great.

Knowing that Greece would become restive on the news of Philip's death, Alexander hurried south. His unexpected arrival probably prevented an Athenian rebellion, but before he could consolidate his hold on Greece, he had to return to the north to deal with Illyrian and Thracian tribes that were threatening his kingdom. The absence of Alexander, followed by later rumours of his death, was enough to cause Thebes to rise up against the Macedonian hegemony in an attempt to regain the leading position it had held in Greece before being supplanted by the power of Philip II.

Again Alexander proved that he would act swiftly and mercilessly toward any opposition. He brought his army south rapidly enough to stop the Theban rebellion from spreading to other states, and then stormed and sacked Thebes itself. Thereafter Alexander's men systematically destroyed the ancient city and threw down its walls. Though attempts were made to revive the city later,

Aristotle, writer, philosopher and tutor of Alexander, as portrayed by Italian painter Francesco Hayez (1791–1882), now in the Gallerie dell'Accademia, Venice.

Thebes never regained more than a shadow of its pre-destruction eminence.

While he had the support of his army, Alexander's position was secure. To keep the soldiers with him, he needed victories – and for these he looked to put into high gear his father's plans for invading the Persian empire. There was another reason for launching this invasion immediately. The army Philip had assembled for the purpose was an expense that Macedon could not long afford. (And indeed, Thebes might have suffered as much as it had because Alexander needed the money he obtained from pillaging the city before it was destroyed.)

In 334 Alexander crossed to Asia Minor accompanied by 12,000 phalangites and 1,800 cavalry. Even with additional lighter-armed auxiliary troops, this was a remarkably compact little army for the task it was intended to accomplish.

Aristotle

A remarkable person who did not join Alexander on his journey east was Aristotle, the king's friend and former tutor. Aristotle possessed one of the most remarkable minds in all antiquity, being interested in ethics, political theory, botany, biology and almost everything else. Though a Greek from Chalcidice (in northeastern Greece), Aristotle's father had served as a doctor in the Macedonian court. Therefore, once Aristotle had served a stint at the Academy of Plato in Athens and travelled extensively in Asia Minor, he readily accepted an invitation to become tutor to the young Alexander in Macedonia.

As tutor to Alexander, the philosopher encouraged the future king's interest in the liberal arts, and also developed within him a lively curiosity about the cultures and creatures of the known world. This led to Alexander later being accompanied on his conquests by a host of scientists who sent a steady stream of botanical samples, geographical reports and other data back to Aristotle.

Staunchly – almost chauvinistically – Greek, Aristotle never understood Alexander's later attempts to fuse the Greek and Persian peoples into a single culture. This led to a degree of estrangement between tutor and former pupil, but Aristotle nevertheless contributed as much to posterity as did Alexander, albeit in a very different way. Not only did Aristotle push forward the boundaries of science in his own day, but he left behind a huge corpus of work for later ages to build upon.

In this Aristotle was aided by the very fusion of Asiatic and Greek culture about which he had so many reservations. After the fall of Rome, his works were almost completely lost to the West. The knowledge he had so painfully accumulated was preserved only in the eastern lands that Alexander had conquered. Rediscovered as a side effect of the Crusades almost 2,000 years after his death, Aristotle and his research were among the major influences behind the Renaissance, which dragged Europe out of the Middle Ages and into the modern era.

The invasion until Granicus

Alexander's first objective was to wrest Anatolia from Persian control. Anatolia – which is today mainly taken up by the nation of Turkey – was a difficult place to conquer because of its hugely diverse geography and mountainous interior. Therefore the correct response by Persia to the Macedonian invasion would have been to exploit the defensive advantages of the terrain and play for time while King Darius mustered his far-flung armies and Alexander ran out of money. Instead, the Persian satraps on the ground decided to bring Alexander to battle and finish his invasion before it got properly started.

The two sides met in battle in May 334 BC on the banks of the River Granicus just north of the Persian provincial capital of Sardis (close to present-day Ergili in Turkey). What exactly happened in this battle is uncertain, partly because the two surviving accounts – by the historians Arrian and Diodorus – are totally incompatible. Roughly, it seems that the Persians opposed the Macedonian attempts to cross the river. When Alexander did get across, it was without his full army, and the Persians launched a determined attempt to end the war by going after Alexander personally. (This was a valid tactic – as demonstrated by the fact that when Alexander became seriously ill the following year, his invasion almost fell apart.)

The attempt to kill Alexander nearly succeeded. He was saved from certain death only by a companion called Cleitus, who cut off the arm of the Persian about to strike the fatal blow. Once the Macedonians finally prevailed, Alexander again showed his intolerance of opposition by ordering the massacre of those Greek mercenaries who had fought against him on the Persian side. Of these 16,000 'traitors', only 2,000 were left alive to be transported in chains back to Greece.

Alexander's destruction of the local Persian army meant that until King Darius could bring up fresh troops from Mesopotamia, the Anatolian Persian provinces of Lydia, Caria and Lycia were defenceless. These quickly fell into Macedonian hands, both securing the western seaboard of Anatolia and doing much to ease

Alexander's cash-flow problems. Famed Greek cities such as Ephesus and Miletus were brought out of Persian control and into the League of Corinth (where the taxes once paid by these cities to the Persian king mutated into compulsory 'voluntary' contributions to defray the expenses of the League).

In a sign of what was to come, Alexander, who had begun by replacing the satraps of conquered Persian provinces with his own henchmen, left Queen Ada of Caria to rule her kingdom once he had captured her capital of Halicarnassus after a four-month siege. Leaving Ada in charge marked the start of Alexander's transition from being head of the Greek League of Corinth to the ruler of an Asiatic Hellenistic empire. In the latter role he would come to rely increasingly on Persian officials and soldiers, and he actively encouraged the fusion of Macedonian and Persian culture among his subordinates. The legendary King Midas had been ruler in Asia Minor, and a prophesy promised the 'rule of Asia' to whomever was able to loose the notoriously complex knot that the king had left tied at his city of Gordium. Alexander famously staked his claim to that rule when he loosed the knot by slicing through it with his sword. Today 'cutting the Gordian knot' has become a metaphor for solving a convoluted problem by the most direct means possible.

Issus and the southward drive

By now Darius, king of kings and ruler of the Persian empire, was well aware of the serious threat posed by Alexander. While Alexander had been consolidating his control of Anatolia, Darius had mustered a huge army and brought it westwards. In this he was helped by the fact that Alexander had spent much of the year debilitated by illness, and until his recovery put him personally in charge once more, his army lacked purpose and direction.

The Persian fleet was self-evidently a threat to the island city-states of the Aegean. Alexander was also haunted by the possibility of a Persian-backed rebellion in Greece. Should that rebellion happen, not only would the Persian fleet cut the supply lines to Alexander's army, but that army would be stranded in Asia Minor, because the Persian fleet would prevent it from returning to Greece.

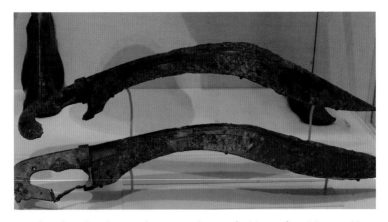

Swords such as these kopis-style weapons (now in the Metropolitan Museum, New York) were secondary to the 12–16 ft (3.7–4.9 m) pikes used by infantrymen in the Hellenistic phalanx.

Furthermore, the Persian fleet could act as a source of supplies in bringing provisions to Darius, who was advancing on Anatolia with an army estimated at between a quarter of a million (by the wildest ancient estimates) and 25,000 men (by the most pessimistic modern assessments). If we assume 100,000 men – as is the modern consensus – then this army would be very hard to feed over the coming winter, and the fleet would be vital to keeping it supplied. Therefore Alexander moved his army toward the Gulf of Issus with the intention of keeping the Persian fleet and Persian army apart from each other.

Whether deliberately or accidentally, Darius took a more northerly route on his way to confront Alexander, and found himself positioned across the Macedonian lines of communication. With both Persians and Greeks cut off from their lines of supply by one another, a confrontation became inevitable. The battle that followed was fought on the banks of the Pinarus river (which river was the Pinarus is now hotly disputed), with mountainous uplands on the Persian left. This conjunction of river and mountains was unfortunate for the Persians because it meant that Darius was unable to bring the full power of his army to bear on a somewhat restricted battlefield.

Perhaps with his experience at the Battle of the River Granicus in mind, Alexander and his infantry drove a break through the

Persian lines. Once he had accomplished this, Alexander joined his companion cavalry and made the battle a very personal affair by going directly after Darius himself. Faced by a homicidal Alexander, Darius turned his chariot and fled the battlefield.

Alexander's move against the enemy commander was a typically daring gamble. By committing so many of his resources to this one endeavour, Alexander had left most of the rest of his army in considerable difficulty. However, with Darius gone, Alexander was able to lend his aid to those troops most in trouble, while morale among the Persians slowly buckled as the news of their monarch's defection spread through the ranks. As always, once a rout started in an ancient army, the true carnage began. With the enemy army comprehensively defeated, Alexander resumed his pursuit of Darius. He was able to cross the river with ease because it was packed with Persian corpses. Darius escaped, but his military treasury fell into Alexander's hands – thus ending Alexander's financial worries once and for all – along with several members of Darius' own family. Alexander treated his captives honourably. However, when Darius

Detail from the Alexander mosaic, showing Alexander confronting Darius in the Battle of Issus. Roman mosaic from Pompeii, now in the Naples National Archaeological Museum.

offered peace in exchange for recognizing Alexander's conquests and the payment of a ransom for his family, Alexander replied that he, the new ruler of Asia, would decide how and if the land was to be divided.

After the victory at Issus, Alexander had the option of driving on to Mesopotamia and the heart of the Persian empire, where Darius had retreated once he had avoided the Macedonian cavalry. However, doing this would leave the Persian fleet menacing the Aegean and Alexander's supply lines. So Alexander turned south toward the Levant with the aim of taking the entire Mediterranean coastline, and so depriving the Persian fleet of a base.

Whether the harsh treatment of those who opposed Alexander was a deliberate strategy to deter resistance or (more probably) a reflection of Alexander's true self, by now this aspect of his character had become well enough known for the Hellenic army to meet with little other than surrender on its southward march. The first serious resistance was encountered at Tyre in what is today the Lebanon. A centre of maritime commerce, Tyre was famous for the 'Phoenician purple' dye that was perhaps the only colour-fast dye for clothing in the ancient world. Tyre was an island city just off the coast, with walls that went right into the sea. Alexander captured the city only after a very difficult siege that lasted seven months, in the course of which his army built a causeway that forever thereafter linked Tyre to the mainland. The usual destruction and massacre that followed resistance accompanied the fall of the city, and thereafter no one dared resist Alexander's southward march until the army came to Gaza, at that time the gateway to the kingdom of Egypt.

The decision of the Persian governor to try to hold Gaza meant that city shared the same fate as Tyre. Thereafter the Persian satrap of Egypt wisely decided that surrender was the better option, so Egypt itself fell into Alexander's hands without a fight. The Persian satrap probably decided not to defend Egypt because the natives bitterly resented the Persian occupation of what had been an independent, often mighty, kingdom for thousands of years. Simultaneously fighting off Alexander and his own rebellious subjects was impossible, and the Persian satrap knew it.

Rather than force his rule upon the Egyptians, as the Persians had done, Alexander concentrated on being accepted by them. He went to great lengths to appease local religious sensibilities and made a long trip into the desert west of the Nile. He did this to duplicate the feat of his alleged ancestor Hercules, who had visited the sacred shrine of Ammon at Siwah. The priests there returned the compliment of the visit by greeting Alexander as the 'Son of Ammon'. The Macedonians considered Ammon to be the name by which the Egyptians worshipped Zeus, king of the gods. Alexander took this as further proof of his mother's allegation that he had been sired on her not by Philip, but by Zeus himself, and therefore he, Alexander, truly was a demi-god.

The event of most lasting significance in this, Alexander's only sojourn in Egypt, was the foundation of the city that still bears his name. Situated on the mainland opposite the island of Pharos, Alexandria had – and has – a sheltered harbour for seagoing ships and easy access to the Nile via nearby Lake Canopus. While Alexander was to found many cities bearing his name (the first had been founded immediately after the Battle of Issus), Egyptian Alexandria was to be his greatest foundation. Home to the later Ptolemaic dynasty, and to the lighthouse that became one of the wonders of the Hellenistic world, for a while Alexandria could claim to be perhaps the greatest city in the Mediterranean world.

Taking an empire

On hearing that Alexander had left Egypt and was preparing to move into the Persian heartlands, Darius made another desperate attempt to make peace. He offered Alexander all his lands west of the river Euphrates, marriage to his daughter and a massive ransom for the rest of his family. On hearing the proposal one of Alexander's advisors, a general called Parmenio, remarked, 'I would accept those terms, if I were Alexander.' To which Alexander snapped back, 'As would I – if I were Parmenio.'

With Alexander set upon the total conquest of Darius' empire, the Persian ruler had no option but to gather his forces for a final confrontation. The decisive battle took place in October 331 BC at

Placido Costanzi, *Alexander the Great Founding Alexandria*, *c.* 1737, oil on canvas.

Gaugamela near the city of Arbela (present-day Arbil) in north-eastern Iraq. At Gaugamela Darius made a determined attempt to avoid the mistakes that had led to defeat on previous occasions. The battlefield was chosen to give maximum advantage to the Persian superiority in manpower and cavalry, and paths were carefully prepared to allow smooth passage to the scythed chariots with which Darius intended to disrupt the ranks of the Hellenic infantry. There were no hills or other defensive features for Alexander to form his army upon, and his supply lines were now so extended that defeat would have been fatal. Yet again, ancient estimates of the size of the Persian army violently disagree with what modern historians consider realistic. Arrian's estimate of a round million – plus 40,000 cavalry – is rejected with contempt, and most modern historians accept an army possibly a tenth that size, or even smaller.

However large it may or may not have been, there is no doubt that the Persian army substantially outnumbered Alexander's. However, apart from an elite bodyguard of 10,000 'Immortals' and a contingent of Greek hoplites prepared to fight to the death after Alexander's treatment of their fellow Greek mercenaries, most of Darius' force lacked training, equipment and morale.

The actual battle was a masterclass in tactical manoeuvre by Alexander. He used his cavalry to force Darius from his prepared position in order to protect his flanks. Broadly, Alexander then used his phalanx as the anvil against which the Persian army was pressed for the hammer-blow inflicted by the Macedonian cavalry. Carrying out this complex battle-plan meant that the phalanx had to withstand intense pressure before the cavalry was ready to strike. Training, discipline and the high morale engendered by so many previous victories made this possible:

> With Darius engaged along the whole battle line, Alexander ordered Aretas to push back the Persian cavalry attempting to get around the right wing of his army, and indeed he himself went off to the right for a short period. But when the cavalry had been pushed back, Alexander turned through the gap left in their ranks. The companion cavalry formed into wedge formation . . . and with a full battle cry Alexander led them in a full-speed charge straight at Darius himself. (Arrian, *Anabasis of Alexander*, 14)

The result replicated the charge at Issus. Darius fled, this time after bitter hand-to-hand fighting, and with his departure the Persian army collapsed. Again there were massive casualties on the Persian side (over 300,000, says Arrian), but this time Darius had no reserves with which to replace them. After Gaugamela, the Persian empire had effectively fallen into Alexander's hands. It was a stunning reversal of the situation 150 years before, when the Greeks at Salamis had been fighting to keep Greece out of the Persian empire. Now, in 331 BC, the Greek empire in Asia was effectively begun.

In recognition of the new order, the three main cities of the Persian empire surrendered to Alexander without a fight. After this demonstration of their new-found loyalty to Alexander, the governors of Susa and Babylon were allowed to keep their positions. In Babylon, as in Egypt, Alexander went to considerable lengths to reconcile the locals to his rule. Among his acts was to order the rebuilding of a temple to Babylon's patron god Marduk, a temple that the Persians had earlier destroyed to punish the Babylonians for a failed rebellion. However, a third imperial city, Persepolis, had no further need of a governor, because, despite its surrender, Alexander destroyed it completely.

The ancient sources suggest that the burning of the city was the result of a drunken courtesan making that suggestion during a celebratory party held by Alexander in the former imperial capital. However, this was clearly not the case. For a start, the archaeological evidence shows that the city appears to have been picked clean of valuables before the destruction, and the population evacuated. Not that there was much of a population to begin with, because Persepolis was a ceremonial and religious site rather than a fully functional city. By destroying it, Alexander sent a message to the world that the Persian empire was no more and that a new kingdom had arisen from its remains. This was most probably his intention all along – a premeditated gesture rather than a drunken impulse.

As a further sign of the changing times, Alexander now represented himself to his new subjects not as a conqueror come to avenge the burning of Athens a century before, but as the avenger of Darius, the last ruler of the Achaemenid line of kings who had ruled the Persian empire for the past two centuries. He was given this opportunity by a treacherous subordinate of Darius who slew his monarch as he fled eastward to prepare for a last stand in Bactria on the eastern fringes of the empire. This subordinate, a man called Bessus, set himself up as the new Persian king. Alexander called on Darius' former supporters to help him against the killer of their former sovereign, and when Bessus was finally captured, Alexander turned him over to Darius' former subjects for punishment and execution.

The capture of Bessus did not end all resistance in the far east of the empire. Alexander ran into an intense rebellion in Sogdiana, a province of the Persian empire just north of Bactria. In part, Sogdiana proved difficult to secure because it lay at the extreme end of Alexander's lines of communication. Its main city was the legendary Samarkand, one of the oldest cities in the world. It gives some idea of the extent of Alexander's new empire that even today the quickest route between Thessaloniki in Greece and Samarkand in

Asia is a fourteen-hour flight covering almost 5,000 kilometres. On this journey the modern traveller overflies Iran and Turkmenistan before touching down in Uzbekistan, several hundred kilometres north of the border with Afghanistan. Few today realize that the entire area covered by this journey was once dominated by the Greeks.

India

Alexander took Samarkand in 329 BC. To further bind the city and province to himself, he married Roxane, a princess with family connections to most of the local nobility. Thereafter, under the Greek name of Macaranda, the city continued to flourish as one of the major stops on the fabulous Silk Road linking China with western Europe. Alexander kept the city as an administrative and military centre, and used it as a base for his next major project.

It is unknown today whether Alexander actually intended to conquer India wholly or in part. What appears certain is that he vastly underestimated the scale of the project and the resources it would require. Already his army had a considerable Persian contingent, because he had discharged many of his veteran Macedonian and Greek soldiers and settled many of them in Sogdiana. It was a further sign of his increasing difficulties with manpower that Alexander relaxed his former harshness toward Greek mercenaries in Asia, and now recruited those he could find into his army.

This army already lacked Alexander's apparently insatiable desire for further conquests, and the proposed Indian adventure filled them with despondency and alarm. Many soldiers had assumed that the eastern expedition had finished with the capture of Persepolis and the death of Darius, and that with the end of the war they would be returning to their distant homes. The fact that Alexander had other plans for them came as an unwelcome surprise.

It did not help that Alexander was becoming increasingly Persian in his mannerisms. Even as his Persian dress and foreign wife appeased the locals, they caused unease among his soldiers. Alexander now required members of his court to perform the

Greek horsemen, as portrayed on the Elgin Marbles.

ritual prostration before their king known as *proskynesis*. To the Persians this was a reassuring symbol that the rituals of life were continuing as before. To the Macedonians it was a sign that power had gone to Alexander's already enlarged head, and they flatly assured him that such arrogance would not be tolerated. Alexander grudgingly gave way, but this minor rebellion among his subordinates increased the paranoia of a man already very intolerant of resistance.

Several plots against Alexander were 'discovered' over the subsequent months, among them a conspiracy among his own pages and another featuring the son of his general Parmenio, one of Alexander's most senior commanders. In 328 BC Alexander and his subordinate Cleitus fell out in a drunken argument about Alexander's pro-Persian policies. The furious Alexander grabbed a javelin and killed Cleitus on the spot, an action for which he was afterwards remorseful, not least because it was that same Cleitus who had saved his life at the Battle of the River Granicus.

Perhaps believing that it would calm everyone's nerves to be back on campaign, in 327 BC Alexander led his army toward the Indus River. His march was essentially a reconnaissance in force, because he knew very little about the subcontinent, and much of what he did believe was wrong. The ostensible purpose behind this foray was to support an Indian king called Taxiles against his neighbours in the area of Kashmir.

It took Alexander some hard fighting through hostile territory even to get to Taxiles, but once his army reached that kingdom their combined strength was enough to force the submission of one of Taxiles' main opponents. The other, King Porus, was a tougher proposition. The major confrontation occurred at the Hydaspes River in 326 BC. Despite taking a strong tactical position and backing up his infantry with a force of two hundred elephants, Porus was outmatched by the tactical skill of Alexander and the experience of his veteran army.

The army of Porus was completely defeated, and Porus himself was captured. When Alexander asked his prisoner how he should be treated, Porus replied 'Like a king.' This reply so delighted Alexander that he not only left Porus in possession of his kingdom but even added to his former captive's domain.

From here Alexander prepared to advance further into India, but his army vehemently disagreed. The monsoon season was beginning, and Alexander's soldiers were not prepared to fight the weather and the population of a subcontinent apparently stocked with an endless supply of soldiers, elephants and cavalry. If Alexander wanted to go on, his soldiers informed him that he was going on alone. They were going home.

Forced to back down, Alexander made arrangements for imperial control of his new possessions along the Indus. He confirmed some rulers in their positions and set up governors from his own retinue in other areas. Thereafter he set off along the coast toward the Persian Gulf, intending his army to co-ordinate its movements with the fleet he was building to establish a Hellenic presence in the Indian Ocean. Alexander intended to take his troops through a notoriously difficult stretch of coastline called Gedrosia, an area in which several previous armies had perished while trying to cross. Alexander got his army back to Persia, but he lost many men on the journey.

Return to Babylon

Alexander marked his return to the heartlands of his new empire with a ferocious purge of many of his former subordinates. Prominent among those who felt his wrath were the satraps and governors of lands through which Alexander had travelled on his return. He felt that not enough had been done to help his army. Even where everything possible had been done to help, Alexander knew that he needed to deflect criticism of his choice of route on to the heads of his unfortunate subordinates.

Others were much more deserving of punishment. While Alexander had been gone some governors had ruled as minor kings, recruiting mercenary armies and diverting tax revenues to their own ends. Among the guilty was an old friend of Alexander's called Harpalus. Harpalus was lame and unable to serve with the army, so Alexander had made him Royal Treasurer. Now, knowing that Alexander was about to discover embezzlement on an epic scale, Harpalus fled with his ill-gotten gains of some seven hundred talents. (Assuming the standard 50 kg gold talent, this comes to approximately U.S.$1.5 billion in 2018 prices – give or take a few hundred million dollars.) Harpalus found refuge in Athens, where the orator Demosthenes was accused of having been bribed to give the embezzler sanctuary.

Given the size of the theft and the depth of his betrayal, there was nowhere in the known world that could protect Harpalus from Alexander's wrath. From Athens Harpalus fled to Crete. There by some accounts he was put to death by his own servants, and by other accounts by a Macedonian adventurer (Pausanias, *Guide to Greece* 2.33). In a nice touch of irony, much of Harpalus' fortune was stolen by the servant whom he trusted to bring it to safekeeping.

Meanwhile Alexander made much of his victories in India, and, following the example of his father, Philip II, who had taken multiple wives, Alexander now further integrated himself into the traditional structure of Persian rule by marrying the daughter of Darius and also a daughter of Artaxerxes III, one of Darius' predecessors. This was done at a grand ceremony at which Alexander also presided over the marriage of many of his officers and thousands of his soldiers, who also took Persian wives.

Despite the disquiet this caused among his veteran troops, it was clear that Alexander intended ultimately to replace his native Macedonians and Greeks with a hybrid Persian-Hellenic army. Already, despite the bitter protests of his men, Alexander had raised a force of 30,000 Persians trained and armed in the Macedonian style. Significantly, he called this unit 'the Successors'. He also made it plain that he expected the offspring of Hellenic soldiers and Persian wives eventually to join his new model army. Though Alexander continued to show the greatest respect to the veterans in his army, their discharge continued and replacements were needed.

There was also a large number of mercenary soldiers in Alexander's empire, many of whom were exiles from mainland Greece. After Alexander had disbanded the private armies of his satraps, many of these men had turned to banditry. He solved the problem, or rather transferred it, by ordering the Greek cities to take back their exiles. The arrival in Greece of large numbers of embittered, unemployed and well-trained soldiers caused considerable disruption and bitterness there toward Alexander, who was now seen as having largely abandoned the ideals of the League of Corinth to set himself up as Persia's new Darius.

Meanwhile there was an ominous development in Alexander's court. His dearest friend, and by many accounts his lover, was a young man called Hephaestion. Alexander liked to compare his relationship with Hephaestion to the legendary companionship of Achilles and Patroclus. As a sign of his favour Alexander married Hephaestion to another of Darius' daughters, thus making the two men family of a sort. Like most of those in Alexander's circle, including Alexander himself, Hephaestion was a heavy drinker, and this probably contributed to his sudden death in 324 BC.

Alexander was distraught and ordered extravagant funeral honours for his deceased companion. When Alexander came to Babylon for part of the funeral ceremonies, his arrival was accompanied by such dire omens that the priests decided the life of Alexander himself was in danger. Alexander disregarded the threat of impending doom and concentrated on Hephaestion's funeral rites and a planned invasion of Arabia. Then he also fell ill after an extended bout of drinking. He fell into a coma from which he never fully emerged. On 10 June 323 BC Alexander, who had conquered more of the planet than anyone before him, and extended the Greek world to the foothills of the Himalayas, the Indus Valley and Egypt, passed away only a month after his 32nd birthday.

The death of Alexander threw much of the world into turmoil, for his rule had been focused on his individual person rather than the institution of the Macedonian kingship, which Alexander had far outgrown. While there were the inevitable rumours of assassination, it is far more probable that Alexander simply burned himself out in a decade and a half of unceasing strain, wounds and

Demosthenes, the Athenian orator, who was a long-standing opponent of Philip II and Alexander. He eventually committed suicide by poison.

forced marches. Modern historians believe that, in the end, a likely attack of malaria combined with an overdose of strong wine to finish off the man whom the myriads of the Persian armies had been unable to kill.

THREE

The Greek Empire

A t the time of his death Alexander was overlord of domains larger than anyone had ruled before – an area of some 9 million square kilometres, or about the area of the continental United States. By way of comparison, the landmass of the Roman empire was just over half that size. To say that Alexander's empire was diverse is to put it mildly. The empire contained thousands of different ethnic and cultural groups and hundreds of different languages.

Herodotus tells a tale by which the Persian king Darius I nicely demonstrated the problems of ruling this diverse empire:

> When Darius was king of Persia, he summoned the Greeks who were at his court. He enquired how much he would have to pay them before they would eat the dead bodies of their fathers. The Greeks replied that there was not enough money in the world.
>
> After that Darius summoned those Indians called the Callatiae. The Greeks remained present and were told what was happening through interpreters. Now the Callatiae actually do eat their parents when they die. So Darius asked them what it would take for them to burn the corpses instead. The Indians cried aloud with horror, and begged that he should not mention so heinous an act. (Herodotus, *History*, 3.38)

In short, the Persian empire was far from being an empire of Persians. Apart from the fact that a Persian – and now a Macedonian

– ruled the whole thing, the different parts of the empire had nothing in common. This is why the emperor Augustus, who was several times the politician Alexander ever was, became intrigued by Alexander's belief that once he had conquered the Persian empire, no comparable challenges remained. Had he, Augustus enquired interestedly, ever tried actually governing what he now possessed?

As a further example of the problems of government, consider that not only did the empire's peoples have different languages, religions and numerical systems, but they could not even agree what day or year it was. The Greek cities alone had each their own calendar. These calendars were roughly aligned with the lunar months, but local politicians were quite happy to add an extra month – for example to extend the summer, or to delay an election. The Egyptians, on the other hand, used the solar year, but as they had not factored in the leap year, their official seasons moved slowly through the calendar. A month that had been spring a century ago was now summer and would be autumn in a few hundred years. The year in any given location depended on the dating system in place. This might be the years since the founding of the city, a year numbered according to the reign of a local king, or some other equally arbitrary system.

Since the newcomers had inherited an empire in which most of the population could not communicate with the rest, and everyone had very different ideas about who they were, how they should be governed and what day and year it was, centralized government was impossible. What Alexander had done was to follow the example of the Persians and simply insert himself at the top of whatever hierarchical system had existed in a society before it was absorbed into the empire.

Consequently, many subject peoples had only a vague idea that they were part of the Persian empire at all, let alone that it had recently changed its top management and become a Graeco-Macedonian empire. Peasants – and over 90 per cent of the population worked in agriculture – continued to till their fields in the traditional way, celebrate their usual festivals and religious rituals, and pay whatever taxes were owed to the headman, chief, Archon or whomever did the collecting. None of this changed.

Hilltop view of Babylon, where Alexander died, and which later became a major city of the Seleucid empire.

In the longer term the fusion of Greek and Eastern culture was to have a major effect on the civilizations of both the West and the Middle East. But in the short term, apart from those areas directly affected by the march of Alexander's armies, for most of its inhabitants the fact that the empire had now changed hands simply did not matter a great deal.

Succession struggles, things fall apart

Alexander was a Macedonian, and as such was well aware of the cut-throat realpolitik and self-serving cynicism with which his fellow aristocrats did their political business. Alexander was young, but he had a very high-risk lifestyle, which meant that he could die at any time. Not despite but because of this, he had been very careful to avoid designating an obvious successor to his rule. Once named, that successor would immediately start scheming to dispose of Alexander before the king changed his mind. The power vacuum at the top following Alexander's death in Babylon was therefore caused by an inherent fault in the Macedonian political system, rather than through poor planning.

That there would be a power struggle after Alexander's death was foreseeable, and if the historian Diodorus Siculus is to believed, that is exactly what Alexander foresaw:

> [Alexander] was dying in Babylon. When he came to his last gasp, his companions asked to whom he was leaving the empire. Alexander replied, 'To the strongest. My funeral games will be the forthcoming huge combat between my friends.' And so it came about, for after Alexander had died his leading companions quarrelled about who should be supreme, and they fought many great conflicts. (*History*, 18.1)

Ostensibly there was a smooth transfer of power from the deceased Alexander to his successor and half-brother Arrhidaeus. However, Arrhidaeus suffered from mental disabilities so severe that he was completely incapable of ruling, so a regent would have to be chosen who would effectively be emperor in all but name. Furthermore, there was already a challenger to the reign of Arrhidaeus, for Alexander's most recent wife, Roxane, was about to give birth to a posthumous child of Alexander. It was agreed that if the child were male (and he was), he would become joint heir with Arrhidaeus.

Ancient mosaic depicting a North African elephant (date unknown). Now extinct, this breed was smaller and more tameable than its sub-Saharan cousins, and less formidable in war than those from India.

Temporarily in charge at the time of Alexander's illness and death was his advisor Perdiccas. Because Perdiccas had the support of leading units of the Macedonian army, he became regent, ruling in the name of the two kings, one an infant and the other mentally disabled. To strengthen his position, Perdiccas decided to marry Alexander's sister Cleopatra, thus alienating one of his leading generals, to whose daughter he had until then been engaged.

As well as juggling marital arrangements, Perdiccas had a lot else to do, for with news of Alexander's death unrest spread through his domain. The Greeks had always disliked being subordinated to Macedon in the League of Corinth, so rebellion could be expected there. Egypt was already in rebellion, having been taken over by a usurper, and Cappadocia in Anatolia – which had never been formally annexed – was now determined to go its own way.

To make things worse, unrest was not limited to the conquered. Once they heard that Alexander was dead, many of the Greek mercenaries, veteran soldiers and others whom he had constrained to settle in distant Bactria made a determined effort to return to their former homes in the west. Perdiccas had to make these settlers to remain in place by the threat of force, yet his own army was mutinous and keen to be disbanded.

The expected rebellion in Greece flared into a short war known as the Lamian War (323–322 BC) after the city of Lamia, around which much of the combat took place. The Athenians led the rebellion and suffered most once it had been crushed, but the rest of Greece also paid the price. The League of Corinth had included Sparta since that city's conquest by one of Alexander's generals in 331 BC. This league was now dissolved, and the southern Greeks became unambiguously Macedonian subjects. That is not to say, however, that the empire Alexander had created was necessarily a Macedonian empire. True, those in command were Macedonian, but the army and the society were pervaded by Greek ideas and culture.

Furthermore, almost before the dust had settled from the conquest of a particular province, a horde of emigrants arrived from the Greek mainland to explore the opportunities opened up by this new frontier. They were joined by expatriates from the hundred or more Greek cities, major and minor, already established on the Asian mainland. In the new cities that sprang up like mushrooms around the empire, the culture was unambiguously Greek. The conqueror was Macedonian, but the world he opened up to the West was from the beginning considered 'Greek'.

The regency of Perdiccas collapsed at the first direct challenge from one of his generals. This general was Ptolemy, a man who knew exactly what he wanted from Alexander's empire and proved ruthlessly single-minded at getting it. Ptolemy had been a childhood friend and loyal subordinate of Alexander, but he felt no loyalty to Perdiccas and the new regime. He moved swiftly to Egypt, allegedly to subdue the independent-minded satrap already there, but in fact to annex the country as his personal fiefdom. In a direct challenge to Perdiccas, Ptolemy hijacked the corpse of Alexander as it was being sent to Macedon for burial, and instead interred the body with great ceremony in Alexandria. Since it fell to a Macedonian king to inter his predecessor, this was a challenge to his authority that Perdiccas could not ignore, especially since Ptolemy had also decided unilaterally to annex the city of Cyrene and the extensive domains under that city's rule.

Perdiccas was never very popular with any but the elite cavalry and bodyguard elements of the army that had given him the regency. Therefore, when Ptolemy proved an astute defender of his new kingdom, the soldiers of Perdiccas refused to face a further long and arduous campaign. Instead they killed their commander and invited Ptolemy to take over the empire.

Wisely, Ptolemy decided that he was content with Egypt. While he and his successors were frequently to joust for power in Syria and the Levant, Egypt itself remained the seat of power for Ptolemy and the dynasty he founded. This continued for the next three centuries, until the Ptolemaic line came to an end with the famous Cleopatra VII, Mark Antony's lover, who committed suicide in 30 BC rather than remain a Roman captive.

It took a while and a few brisk mini-wars before a division of power was formalized in 311 BC. At that time a peace settlement was agreed among the surviving generals of Alexander. By these terms Ptolemy would remain nominally a subordinate of the Macedonian

Map showing the Hellenistic kingdoms, *c.* 275 BC.

kings. The royal (but not ruling) pair were now installed in Macedon under the new regent, Antipater. Asia was left to another powerful and ambitious general, Antigonus Monophthalmus – the One-eyed – who ruled with the aid of his energetic and capable son Demetrios. Just as this regime was settling in, Antipater complicated matters by dying and throwing everything into chaos once more. Cassander, his son, took power, but it soon became apparent that his authority was not acknowledged beyond Macedon's European possessions.

Then in 310 BC Alexander's son by Roxane died, and the pretence that Alexander's dynasty still ruled a united empire became even more threadbare. Antigonus now saw himself as the man to reunite all of Alexander's fractured empire under his rule. Consequently, in 307 BC he sent an army under his son to 'free' Greece from the rule of Cassander. Demetrios threw himself into the task. He became so adept at capturing cities that he was given the name Demetrios Poliorcetes – Demetrios the Besieger. A string of victories, including the 'liberation' of Athens, led to the men of the army spontaneously declaring Antigonus to be their king. Ptolemy quickly took the title for himself also, and Cassander and several other generals who had likewise seized autonomous territories in Alexander's former empire did the same. That empire was now formally split into the different kingdoms that were to become known as the Hellenistic world.

The shaping of the new world

The ever-increasing power of Antigonus had the natural result of drawing his opponents into a coalition against him. The struggle came to its climax in 301 BC, when Antigonus and Demetrios faced their principal rivals, the generals Lysimachus, Ptolemy and Seleucus. The Battle of Issus was decided by the elephants of Seleucus, which prevented the Antigonid cavalry from rejoining the main army. Antigonus himself was killed in the battle and Demetrios, who fled the battlefield, was reduced to the role of king without a kingdom. The victors divided Antigonus' realm among them. Lysimachus took control of Anatolia, and Seleucus got Syria and points east (although Bactria was already slipping out of his control). The ever-opportunistic Ptolemy grabbed possession of the Levant while Seleucus was too weak to prevent him and everyone else was too distracted.

Matters remained in this uneasy equilibrium for almost a quarter of a century. Demetrios added spice to the period by an opportunistic takeover of Macedon after the death of Cassander, but he was quickly ousted from power by Lysimachus and King Pyrrhus of Epirus (the same Pyrrhus who was later to invade Italy in an unsuccessful attempt to supplant the rising power of Rome). Demetrios finished his days as a prisoner of Seleucus, who took advantage of Lysimachus' distraction in Macedon to invade Anatolia. Lysimachus died on the battlefield, but the victorious Seleucus was assassinated almost before he could enjoy his triumph. With his death the last chance of reuniting the empire of Alexander slipped away, and the rough division of the spoils of his conquest assumed the shape it would retain for the next three hundred years.

In the east was Bactria, an ostensibly Greek kingdom that had much tighter links with India and the kingdoms of Central Asia than with mainland Greece or Macedon. Communication between Bactria and the rest of Alexander's former empire was

Dromedary and camel wrangler, from an early imperial Roman bas-relief now in the Vatican Museum.

difficult and accomplished mainly through trade along the Silk Road. The Greeks in Bactria had as little interest in the power struggles on the Mediterranean coast as the western Greeks had in the complex political game in the Ganges Valley. Inevitably, over the next century Bactria began to drift out of the Hellenistic orbit to become a separate kingdom with a fusion of Greek and eastern cultures.

West of Bactria were the lands ruled by the heirs of Seleucus. This rump of Alexander's domains was large enough to deserve the title of 'empire' in its own right, and it has since been known as the Seleucid empire. The Seleucid rulers kept possession of Anatolia, which their founder had won from Lysimachus, but had only nominal control of the interior. The highlands of Anatolia became the separate kingdom of Galatia, thanks to a massive invasion of western Gauls, who eventually settled there after bouncing about destructively through the lands around the western Black Sea. (It was to these Gauls that

St Paul several centuries later wrote the letter preserved in the Bible as the Letter to the Galatians.)

South of the Seleucid empire was the Ptolemaic kingdom of Egypt. The northern border of this kingdom was to shift depending on the relative strength of the Ptolemaic and Seleucid rulers, but everything south of Gaza was and remained Ptolemaic; a self-sufficient kingdom centred on Alexandria, which was soon to become a beacon of Hellenistic civilization.

To the west were Macedonia and Greece. The original home of the conquerors of Asia now struggled to compete with the successor states, which considerably outmatched it in money and resources. It did not help that Macedonian rulers had to be increasingly heavy-handed to maintain their tenuous hold on Greece, and this resulted in the large-scale emigration of the most energetic and enterprising Greeks to the new kingdoms and opportunities in the east. Other Greeks fled westward, but the cities of Magna Graecia were also falling under the control of a sovereign nation-state. This was Rome, which advanced southwards down the Italian peninsula, conquering Greek cities such as Capua and Naples and absorbing them into its growing empire.

The Hellenistic world and the new era

Even with the influx of Greeks from the European mainland, the eastern Greeks were a small minority in their new empire. It might have been expected that over a relatively brief period these Greeks would be rapidly absorbed into the native population, leaving little trace of their invasion other than some Western influence on art and perhaps the occasional blue-eyed child. This did not happen, and the reason was that at this time Greek culture had a lot to offer the rest of the world.

PHILOSOPHY

The legacy of the fifth-century intellectual revolution meant that the Greek way of looking at the universe stimulated and provoked the many cultures with which it interacted. Greek intellectual ideas were

The verses of poets such as Callimachus were designed to be recited to the accompaniment of a lyre – which is why the words to modern songs are called 'lyrics'.

debated and absorbed into the cultural systems and belief frameworks of other cultures, which in turn fed their ideas back into the patterns of Greek thought. Many of the ideas and philosophies that we regard as classically Greek in fact emerged from this intellectual fusion of the Hellenistic era. Some of these philosophies exist today as words that briefly sum up the qualities they embodied.

For example, the original 'Stoic' was a Cypriot called Zeno, who founded the school of Stoic philosophy in 300 BC. Zeno originally taught in Athens, in the porch (*stoa* in Greek) of one of the public buildings in the *agora*. (The *agora* was the commercial and administrative centre of a Greek city. The crowds and bustle in such places has given the fear of them the name of 'agoraphobia'.) However, his ideas spread far beyond that city, and later developments in Stoic thought were driven by schools in the Seleucid and Ptolemaic kingdoms, such as those in Tarsus and Alexandria respectively. Stoicism encouraged its followers to concentrate on developing the self and to scorn the ups and downs of external fortune. To the Stoics, any man was free who considered himself as such, since no external force could compel a man who was not prepared to submit to it. By this argument slavery was chosen freely by those who did not feel that death was the better option, so Stoics had little interest in freeing slaves (though they felt that slaves should be treated well). Indeed, in a later era, one of the greatest Stoic philosophers of ancient Rome was Epictetus, a former slave from Asia Minor. Even later, another Stoic was Marcus Aurelius, emperor from AD 161 to 180.

Another group, the Epicureans, expanded on the theories of the classic Atomist school. They believed that the combination of atoms that formed the body was broken up upon death, and that nothing remained after that dissolution. Therefore the Epicurean philosophy concentrated on having its adherents make the most of life while they had it, and for this reason an 'Epicurean' today is considered a connoisseur of good food, fine wine and the arts.

The Skeptics were, well, sceptical. They considered that everything we perceive as fact was actually either totally false, or at best only a fraction of the true reality. Furthermore, the Skeptics despaired of ever discovering the true reality. (This concept has regained traction in the modern era, when it has been shown that humans and their limited senses do indeed appreciate only a fraction of the reality about them, and anyway it is statistically probable that the entire universe as we know it exists only as a computer simulation.)

Rather than reject reality as a whole, the Cynics rejected civilization and its artificial constraints on behaviour. For this reason they received their contemptuous name, which comes from the word 'dog', or *cynos* in Greek. The founder of this movement was also from Asia Minor, Diogenes of Sinope. Diogenes was a contemporary of Alexander the Great, who is said to have visited the philosopher while both were in Corinth:

> Alexander found him [Diogenes] lying stretched out in the sunshine. When he saw a great throng of people arriving, he looked up and saw Alexander standing over him. Alexander gave his greetings and asked what was in his power to do for Diogenes. Diogenes replied, 'Well, you could stand aside a bit. You are getting in the way of my sun.' . . . Later Alexander remarked, 'Say what you like. If I were not Alexander, I would like to be Diogenes.' (Plutarch, *Life of Alexander*, 14)

In the years after Alexander's death, Greek philosophy evolved into Hellenistic philosophy, the distinction being that many of the philosophers involved were neither Greek nor living in Greece. Actually, some of the later tales about Zeno the Stoic suggest that he was of Phoenician stock.

SCIENCE

The Greek discovery of empiricism meant that philosophy was far from an abstract concept. It was in the Hellenistic era that science got started properly as an intellectual discipline. The Greeks called it *epistemonikos*, literally 'manufacturing knowledge'. Although most Greek science consisted of observing natural phenomena and drawing conclusions from these observations, a few enterprising souls decided to change the conditions under which these phenomena occurred, and observe what difference this made to the outcome. These were among the first experiments done for no practical purpose other than to acquire knowledge.

What is interesting about the science of the Hellenistic era – which is considered to be the period of greatest scientific development in history before the Enlightenment in the seventeenth century of the modern era – is how scattered were the foci of scientific achievement. Archimedes in Syracuse built on the work of scientists in Alexandria, who in turn learned from those from Pergamon in Asia Minor, who had obtained data from Babylon in Mesopotamia. Science was international, but Hellenic.

Among those who worked with Babylonian astronomical data was Aristarchus of Samos (310–230 BC). Aristarchus was the first to postulate that the Earth and planets orbited the sun, a concept so evidently ridiculous that the idea was shelved for another eighteen hundred years. Later Archimedes was among those who shot down the notion because the newly discovered concept of parallax proved that for Aristarchus' idea to work, the stars would have to be thousands of millions of miles away. Aristarchus himself had taken this concept on board. He had observed that more distant objects seem to move more slowly. From this he deduced that stars that appear fixed in the heavens are indeed actually moving, but are incredibly far away. Therefore, from his unique perspective, parallax was not a problem.

Another contemporary scientist who was far ahead of his time was Herophilos of Chalcedon. Born in Asia Minor, Herophilos moved to Ptolemy's Alexandria, where he set up a school of medicine. He was one of the first to study anatomy practically through dissection, and he made a sporting attempt to discover the purpose of the different areas of the human brain. Where previous belief made the heart the seat of the intellect, Herophilos established that it was the brain.

It was also Herophilos who named the duodenum, the small intestine below the stomach that is twelve fingers (*duodeka daktulon*) in length. It was an example of Ptolemy's forward-thinking nature that Herophilos was able to carry out dissections at all, for in most of the world the dissection of corpses was illegal. In Alexandria

Herophilos often worked in the open so that the public could attend his dissections and hear his commentary.

The work of Herophilos is now lost and has survived only through comments by later writers such as the Roman doctor Galen. According to the Church Father Tertulian, Herophilos also vivisected living prisoners, but Tertulian was writing much later and was bitterly opposed to almost everything Herophilos did and stood for, so the veracity of his statement is dubious. On the other hand, Herophilos did work out that the heart was a pump, something best established by close observation of that organ in action. He also discovered that only blood flowed in arteries, and not a mix of blood and air, as Aristotle had supposed. (However, Aristotle was correct in assuming that the arteries carried air to the limbs. It was just that no one had yet figured out how oxygen and haemoglobin worked together.)

Euclid was unusual among the bevy of distinguished scientists described here, for of all the 'Greek' philosophers and scientists mentioned he is the only one who was actually born in Greece, in the city of Megara. However, he swiftly remedied this by moving to Alexandria as a young man. Unlike Herophilos, whose work was messily practical, Euclid operated on the more austere plane of mathematics. While we know almost nothing of Euclid's life, the world is very familiar with his work. He wrote a book on geometry so comprehensive that it became the standard work on the subject and tortured schoolchildren for the next 2,000 years – the longest any single textbook has remained in print. A study of Euclid's number theory, for example the correlation between perfect numbers and Mersenne primes, will do much to disperse any idea that the Hellenistic Greeks were either primitive or unsophisticated.

It is no coincidence that so many of the great names mentioned above worked in Alexandria or were influenced by the research being done there. Ptolemy tried hard to attract a constellation of the finest minds in the Hellenistic world to his new capital. This was both for practical purposes – he realized quickly that science offers practical benefits to a ruler who embraces it – and for propaganda reasons, to demonstrate that Egypt was now a Hellenic state.

This figurine from Ptolemaic Egypt shows a remarkable fusion of symbols from the Egyptian goddess Isis (such as a knotted dress) and the Greek Athena (a helmet).

One of Ptolemy's recruits for this purpose was a former governor of Athens, a man called Demetrios of Phaleron. This Demetrios had been installed as governor by Cassander of Macedon (see above) and exiled in 307 BC during the tumultuous period when Demetrios the son of Antigonus the One-eyed invaded Greece. Demetrios of Phaleron was recruited by Ptolemy because as well as being a politician, he was an outstanding orator and had written extensively on rhetoric, literary criticism and history.

It is probable that at this point Ptolemy was already mulling the idea of creating the famous Library of Alexandria, which was to become the foremost beacon of learning throughout the remainder of antiquity. Many historians believe that the multitalented Demetrios was charged by Ptolemy with the task of getting this library off the ground, and also with updating the Egyptian legal code. Certainly the foundation of the Library is contemporary with Demetrios' later years in Alexandria, and the institution was already a going concern in the reign of Ptolemy's successor.

Following the example of Ptolemy, the Seleucids established a centre of learning at the newly founded city of Antioch (named by Seleucus after his son Antiochus) and, not to be outdone, the Macedonians established their own centre at the city of Pella.

The Greek view of the world as a machine could not help but affect how other religions perceived the cosmos. Heretofore there had been little point in trying to make sense of the world because things were as they were because the gods had made them so, and things happened because the gods had decreed that they should. The Greeks did not disagree, but looked at the matter more closely. Thus a pious Greek was prepared to admit that Poseidon caused earthquakes and tsunamis, but he was also prepared to wonder how Poseidon managed the latter. The historian Thucydides, for example, deduced correctly that earthquakes caused tsunamis because they abruptly changed the level of the seabed. Modern scientists would not disagree, other than to suggest that it was not Poseidon 'the earth-shaker' who was the motivating force.

Likewise, the Greek view was that their gods were sentient forces of nature (Zeus was the god of order, Aphrodite the goddess of love, Iris the goddess of the rainbow, and so on). This made it easy for peoples of other cultures to see aspects of their gods in the Greek versions, and in a process called syncretism, otherwise very different religious beliefs and practices were blended into a common religious framework. Ultimately the process went furthest in the Roman empire, where the Greek and Roman gods were seen as exactly the same deities, albeit with different names.

While the Greeks were successful in spreading the worship of their gods about the Mediterranean and Middle East, they in turn accepted several different gods into their pantheon, including Isis and Serapis from Egypt. (Worship of the latter god was strongly promoted by Ptolemy, who saw the advantages of a shared Graeco-Egyptian god unifying his people.) It was also at this time that the worship of Attis, a god from Phrygia in Asia Minor, began to spread through the Hellenistic world.

The Greek culture of the Hellenistic states became a common attribute, which made it easier for people to move around. It was not only the Greeks who took advantage of this. Alexandria rapidly built up a large Jewish population. Within a generation many of these Jews were more fluent in Greek than in their native Hebrew, and this led to the translation of the Books of Moses into Greek. This was a major step in making Judaism accessible to a wider audience, and this pioneering translation is today still known as the Septuagint after the seventy scholars who worked on it.

Greek philosophy explained that the universe did not require constant hands-on supervision by the gods. This caused some philosophers, including Epicurus, to suggest that the gods were less interested in human affairs than had previously been believed. However, there were 'gods' close at hand as well. The Greek view

Sarcophagus of a woman from Magna Graecia, now in the Guarnacci Museum, Volterra.

was that a man of truly exceptional ability could so far surpass the bounds of humanity that he (at this time it was invariably a 'he') could literally become divine.

As a result, it became common for the Hellenistic rulers to be worshipped as gods. While this seems like the most cynical of flattery to modern eyes, it must be understood that there was nothing in Greek religious belief that flatly contradicted this possibility – not least because even the most traditional of Greek gods had a distressingly human collection of weaknesses, failings and foibles. Consequently the divine worship accorded Hellenistic rulers was sometimes genuine and sincere, albeit approaching the concept of divinity from a very different direction to that of modern thought on the topic.

LITERATURE

While science progressed by leaps and bounds, literature and the arts developed more slowly. This is not because the age was devoid of writers – one Kallimachos of Cyrene is alleged to have written more than eight hundred books – but because a reverence for the great works of the past meant that those of a literary disposition were more likely to be employed codifying the writings of Homer than in producing their own works.

Kallimachos himself is a good example. He was born in Cyrene during the reign of Ptolemy, and was a fine scholar during the reign of Ptolemy's successor, Ptolemy II (Philadelphus). Many of his eight hundred books were literary criticism or bibliographic surveys of what had already been written by whom. When it came to his own productive work, Kallimachos ensured that his verses were short and to the point, in keeping with the spirit of his attacks on the long-winded poetry of yore.

Poetry was perhaps the foremost literary form of the era, and the Hellenistic age produced works that easily stand comparison with those of earlier eras. By now it comes as no surprise to discover that the leading poets of the early Hellenistic period flourished in Alexandria under the patronage of Ptolemy.

Many an aspen, many an elm, bowed and rustled overhead,
Close by, the sacred water splashed from the cave of the
    nymphs,
While the brown cricket busily chirped in the leafy branches,
And the tree-frog murmured high in the dense thorn-brake.
The lark sang, and the goldfinch sang, the turtle-dove moaned,
And the springtime bees hummed and hovered to and fro.

This is an extract from the *Idylls* of Theocritus (Idyll 7, l. 135). Theocritus was one of the first poets to abandon heroic and sacred themes to concentrate on an idealized depiction of country life that has given this style of poetry the name 'bucolic'. Little is known of his life, other than that he evidently had strong connections to Magna Graecia in general and Syracuse in particular. His work went on to strongly influence the Roman poets Virgil and Horace, and through them the Romantic poets of the eighteenth century.

Theatre was the one field in which Athens remained supreme, thanks to the work of the playwright Menander (342–290 BC). His works were light-hearted plays on enduring social themes in the context of his times – love, marriage, annoying neighbours and moral dilemmas. This was in stark contrast to the highly political satires of Menander's comic predecessor Aristophanes. While the style of the 'Old Comedy' that Aristophanes embodied mercilessly flayed politicians and public figures (including Socrates) with vivid, often highly obscene verses, the 'New Comedy' of Menander was more mannered. He seldom ventured even veiled criticism of the powers that be.

Menander's rival Philemon was a Greek from Syracuse who moved to Athens to practise his art. Like many of his contemporaries, Philemon was attracted to Alexandria, but returned to Athens after a brief sojourn in Egypt. Philemon's works have survived less well than Menander's, and even Menander's plays are mostly fragmentary, or survive only as isolated speeches and quotations. Philemon's main contribution to posterity was himself, for he lived for about a hundred years, surviving through the entire first third of the Hellenistic era.

An Athenian woman from the era of Pericles makes an offering to the gods. She is in typical dress, but note the hint of rich embroidery on the sleeves.

FOUR

THE HELLENISTIC WORLD FROM EAST TO WEST

B y the start of the second century BC, an inhabitant of the ancient world would have been unsurprised to meet a Greek anywhere between the Himalayan mountain range and the Atlantic coast of Iberia. Nor would our hypothetical inhabitant have been taken aback if that Greek told him that he had come from a Greek city situated nearby. Even outside the Hellenistic kingdoms, the Greek people and their culture were widely – if thinly – spread around the ancient world. In the next two chapters we will look in more detail at the Greek settlements of the Hellenistic era, their extent, their culture and their impact, both on the people of the lands where the Greeks became established and the effect of that settlement on future eras.

One of the great advantages of the strength of Hellenistic culture was that it acted as a unifying force for Greeks wherever they were. A Greek from Egypt and a Greek from Spain could meet in Italy and discuss the plays of Sophocles, which both would have viewed in remarkably similar theatres and heard in a common tongue. In fact, the version of Greek in use throughout the Mediterranean and beyond was called *Koine*, which means 'common'. Even non-native Greeks learned the language because it helped – for example – Syrians in the Seleucid empire to communicate with Paphlagonians and others among that empire's linguistically diverse population.

In some areas, Hellenism was a pervasive influence that forever changed the culture of those peoples with whom it interacted. This was because, as the Macedonian rulers of the Hellenistic kingdoms identified themselves as Greek, it rapidly dawned on the local elites that the more Greek they became, the better were their chances of advancement under the new regime. As a result the cultural trend-setters in areas ruled by Hellenistic monarchs largely abandoned, or at least dramatically modified, their customary behaviour. The traditional beliefs and practices in such regions were increasingly confined to 'backward' rural areas and the peasantry. The extent to which this happened is best shown by the people who most strenuously resisted cultural assimilation – the Jews.

The people of Judaea had spent millennia grimly holding on to their particular way of life. They had resisted attempts to change them by Assyrians, Egyptians and Persians, yet even in this most stubborn of cases, some were swayed by the charms of Hellenistic culture. The Book of Maccabees in the Septuagint gives a good, if highly biased, view of the struggle:

> There emerged in Israel a forsworn group who led many people astray. 'Look,' they said, 'we should ally ourselves with the Gentiles surrounding us. Numerous calamities have overtaken us since we separated ourselves from them.'
>
> This idea was widely accepted and many people petitioned the [Seleucid] king who allowed them to conduct themselves in the way of the Gentiles. In Jerusalem they built a gymnasium, such as Gentiles have. They hid their circumcision, abandoned the holy covenant and became willing servants of sacrilege by submitting to Gentile rule. (1:11–15)

While in Israel the cultural clash degenerated into actual warfare, in other areas assimilation happened quietly and unremarked. Elsewhere, especially in those areas deep within the hinterland beyond the coastal cities, life went on much as before. Even those who did make it that far inland were seen not as cultural game-changers, but simply as another thread to be added to the rich fabric of local tradition. This became the case with Bactria and the eastern Greeks more than with any others.

Bactria

Today many know of Bactria only through its most readily identified native species: the two-humped Bactrian camel. These animals
– a small number of which still roam wild in their native habitat –
were domesticated thousands of years before the Greek conquest
of the region. For merchants moving goods along the Silk Road,
the Bactrian camel was a godsend. A strong, fit member of this
hardy species is able to cope with extremes of temperature and a
poor diet and yet still carry loads of up to 250 kilograms almost
50 kilometres per day.

As has already been mentioned, much of the wealth of Bactria
came from the fact that it sat at the intersection of the Indian and
Persian civilizations and could channel to both areas goods from
China and beyond. (Even in this period, spices grown in Java ended
up being ground over Ptolemaic dinners in Egypt, though by then
the product had passed through the hands of so many middlemen
that both Javanese growers and Greek consumers were unaware
of each other's existence.)

Ancient Bactria was a land of contrasts. While the exact political
boundaries were often in flux, the geographical extent of the land
can be defined as lying between the Hindu Kush mountains in the
south and the Oxus River to the north. Between the Oxus and the
mountains is a fertile strip running east to west alongside the foothills of the Hindu Kush range, with a band of arid terrain merging
into desert south of the Oxus River.

The religion of the area was the worship of the Fire God,
Ahura-Mazda. The current form of the religion was that handed
down by the prophet Zarathustra, and had much in common
with later religions such as Christianity. As with the Christian
faith, the Zoroastrian religion is basically monotheistic, involving
belief in a supreme God, his evil counterpart and a judgement
of the followers of both at an apocalyptic End of Days. Perhaps
because of its similarity to the Abrahamic faiths of Judaism,
Christianity and Islam, followers of Zarathustra have been per-
secuted with particular fervour by the last two religious groups.
Nevertheless, Zoroastrianism spread to the west through the

Hellenistic empires of the time, and there it has had a tenuous foothold ever since.

It was probably his initial failure to understand the Zoroastrian religion that led to Alexander's difficulties in Bactria. The local belief that burial defiled the ground and that burning corpses impiously violated the sanctity of fire meant that the usual Greek methods of disposing of their dead caused outrage among the natives. It did not help that Alexander underestimated the extent of the ties that bound the people of Bactria to the land of Sogdiana to the north. Alexander's attempt to divide the area into two economic and administrative regions led to a four-year revolt. Once this was finally crushed, Alexander went to the opposite extreme and settled Bactria-Sogdiana as a single satrapy with Samarkand as the regional centre in the north and the city of Bactra (present-day Balkh) in the south.

Alexander's settlement of some 30,000 veterans in the satrapy was not the first Greek presence in the area, for under the Persian empire recalcitrant rebels from Ionian Greek cities had been settled wholesale in the region by King Darius I. These first Greeks thought of themselves as exiles, and Alexander's soldier-settlers were none too happy with their lot either. As we have seen, on Alexander's death they attempted to emigrate en masse. The attempted emigration was stopped by force of arms that killed some of the settlers. Thereafter Bactria remained so far out of contact with the West that the land was considered almost foreign territory when it was re-invaded by the army of Seleucus in 308 BC and briefly rejoined to the Seleucid domains.

According to the later geographer Strabo, at this point Seleucus negotiated with an Indian king the exchange of some of his Bactrian holdings for five hundred elephants. These were the elephants that were later instrumental in the defeat of Antigonus the One-eyed at the battle of Issus.

In 245 BC a people called the Parni overran the eastern portion of the Seleucid empire and established a kingdom that over the centuries would grow first to rival and then eventually to overwhelm the Seleucids. The rise of Parthia placed a non-Greek kingdom and culture squarely between Greek Bactria and the West.

Statuette of a rider wearing an elephant scalp. This is possibly the 3rd-century king Demetrios I of Bactria.

Unsurprisingly, from this period onwards, the culture of Bactria grew ever more eastern even as the actual details of its history become increasingly vague.

Though cut off from the West, Bactria lost none of its vigour. The kingdom began to interact ever more closely with the Indian states to the south through conquest, trade and diplomacy. Much of the Bactrian north ceased to be Greek in the 180s BC, when the area was overwhelmed by invading nomadic tribes, but by then the Bactrians had expanded well to the south. The result was an entity known either as the Indo-Greek kingdom or the Graeco-Bactrian kingdom. Archaeology has shown that the kings in this period continued to produce coins that were virtually indistinguishable from their Western counterparts, and art and sculpture retained a clear Western influence even centuries later, when most of the hybrid-Greek population had converted to Buddhism.

In fact the combination of Greek and Indian influences gave rise to an art form known today as Gandhara art. This flourished in the region for almost a thousand years, until the Muslim conquest of the 7th century AD. Among the last but best-known products of this Graeco-Buddhist fusion were the famous Buddhas of Bamiyan, monumental statues that were carved into sandstone cliffs and infamously dynamited by Taliban religious fanatics in 2001.

The Seleucid empire until 222 BC

To the west of Bactria lay the Seleucid empire, which was perhaps the most important political entity in the Mediterranean world until the rise of Rome. The empire takes its name from its founder, Seleucus I Nicator, one of Alexander's generals. Of all the *diadochi* (as the successors to Alexander were known), Seleucus had the most difficult road to power. The lands he later came to rule were originally held by Perdiccas, and after his death briefly by Antipater, who passed on his rule to the aggressively ambitious Antigonus the One-eyed. Seleucus, originally the very competent governor of the province of Babylon, fell out with Antigonus soon after the latter took power, and was forced to flee for shelter to Ptolemy of Egypt.

With the power of Antigonus growing ever more threatening, Seleucus was foremost in organizing the coalition that finally took on the challenge of reining in the expansionist Antigonus. While Antigonus and his rivals squared off for battle near Gaza, Seleucus was sent with a small force to regain his former command in Babylon, where his rule was fondly remembered. With Babylon as his base, Seleucus promptly set about enlarging his possessions and converting himself from a Ptolemaic client to a king in his own right. As we have seen, his campaigns in the east helped him to claim resources that were later deployed against Antigonus in the west. The historian Appian describes how Seleucus thereafter took advantage of his position to become perhaps the most powerful of the successor kings:

Once Antigonus had been slain in battle, the confederated kings who had helped Seleucus destroy Antigonus set about dividing his domains. The portion of Seleucus ran through Syria from the Euphrates [river] to the sea and inland to Phrygia.

By force of arms or the persuasion of diplomacy, Seleucus patiently waited for each opportunity to extend his rule to his neighbours. In this way he became ruler of Mesopotamia, Armenia and Cappadocia, and also [the nations of] the Persians, Parthians, Bactrians, Arians and Tapurians, Sogdianans, Arachosians, Hyrcanians, and all other peoples as far as the Indus [river] whom Alexander had conquered in war.

As a result he ruled more of Asia than any ruler apart from Alexander – everything from Phrygia eastwards to the river Indus was under his power. He even crossed the Indus and made war on the Indian king Sandracottus [Chandragupta Maurya] about that river boundary, a war which was eventually settled by a treaty of friendship and a marriage alliance. (*History of the Syrian Wars*, 11.55)

While still a general of Alexander, Seleucus had considered returning to his native Macedon. As was usual for a Greek of his day who was contemplating a lengthy journey, Seleucus had consulted an oracle to ensure that the trip would go smoothly. In fact, the oracle proved dead set against the journey. It advised Seleucus, 'Do not hasten to Europe. Asia is much better for you.'

As a result Seleucus did not return to his homeland until he was in his seventies. By that time he had transferred much of his empire into the control of his son Antiochus. He then took his army to extend the rest of his empire westwards into Thrace. Along the way Seleucus picked up Ptolemy's elder son (Ptolemy Ceraunus), who had stormed out of Egypt when it became clear that Ptolemy intended his second son, Ptolemy Philadelphus, to succeed him.

A skilled general, Seleucus defeated his enemies and seemed about to add Thrace and Macedonia to his domains. At that point he was treacherously slain by Ceraunus to whom he had given shelter, probably because the assassin saw a chance to seize the

Macedonian kingdom for himself. Justice was not long delayed, because although young Ptolemy successfully seized control of Macedonia and Greece, he was soon thereafter defeated, captured and beheaded by invading Galatian tribesmen. Nevertheless, the assassination of Seleucus meant that the western border of the Seleucid realm never extended further west than the Hellespont. Macedon remained an independent kingdom.

The two main capitals of the Seleucid empire were Antioch in Syria and Seleucia-on-the-Tigris, both founded by Seleucus and intended to act as twin foci for the western and eastern parts of his empire. However, the attention of Seleucus' successors was mainly on the west, which was one reason why the east slowly drifted out of Seleucid control. Antiochus I had to deal with scattered rebellions almost as soon as news of his father's assassination became public. He suppressed a revolt in Syria, but was less successful in Asia Minor. Here the independent and bloody-minded Cappadocians again successfully asserted their independence after being briefly and tenuously absorbed into the Seleucid domains. To the northwest, Bithynia now became an independent kingdom on the Anatolian coast.

Perhaps to distract the attention of the Seleucid armies, the Bithynian ruler, Nicomedes, invited the marauding Galatian tribesmen to make themselves at home in Anatolia. The Galatians, who were at that time being roughly handled in Macedonia, took up the offer in 278 BC. In Anatolia the invading barbarians caused considerable disruption and loss of life before they were confronted by Antiochus and his army three years later. The Galatians had never previously come across war elephants, which, as at Issus thirty years before, proved key to the victory. The Galatians were thenceforth confined to the arid uplands of the Anatolian interior, and there they remained for the rest of antiquity. Nevertheless, from the point of view of Nicomedes of Bithynia, the distraction succeeded, and the Seleucid armies were unable to prevent his kingdom from becoming firmly established.

Despite victory over the Galatians, the Seleucid empire was fraying. The sheer diversity and geographical extent of the empire made it virtually impossible for any one man to hold it all together.

Antiochus tried the obvious solution of putting the eastern part of his domains under the control of a viceroy, in this case his eldest son. This solution had the equally obvious failing that the son quickly decided that he preferred to be an independent monarch. However, the cautious Antiochus had been keeping an eye on his son, and had him executed for treason before his plans to become a breakaway king came to fruition.

Much of the rest of Antiochus' twenty-year reign was spent moving up and down his kingdom dealing with wars and rebels. There was constant friction with Egypt owing to the ambitions of the Ptolemies in the area known as Coele-Syria, which was basically the southern Levant and Gaza. Having seized the area in a war in 301 BC, the Ptolemies held it against strong Seleucid pressure and periodically attempted to extend their power further to the north. Pergamon, a neighbour of breakaway Bithynia, had never been a part of Seleucus' domains, though that monarch had stridently insisted that it was. Antiochus spent the last years of his life attempting to assert his father's claims, probably as a preliminary to reclaiming Bithynia, but he died with that ambition unrealized shortly after suffering a defeat at Pergamene hands near Sardis.

The next Seleucid king, Antiochus II, seemed destined to share his father's career as an imperial fireman, as wars and rebellions flared up through the empire. It was while Antiochus II was preoccupied with yet another interminable war with Egypt that the Parni took the opportunity to establish the Parthian kingdom in the Seleucid hinterlands and so cut Bactria off from the west. This forced Antiochus to attempt diplomacy and a disastrous foray into dynastic politics with the Ptolemies.

To collect resources for war against the Parthians, Antiochus II needed peace with the Egyptians. Therefore he agreed to marry the Ptolemaic princess Berenice, and agreed that any children of that union would inherit the Seleucid empire. In return he received an enormous dowry, perhaps to compensate him for the fact that his new marriage necessitated the repudiation and exile of his current wife, Laodice, together with her children. Laodice did not take this development well, and immediately began scheming to regain her former position. It helped that her ex-husband had a predilection for holding drunken parties at which he allegedly became intimate with his young male guests, conduct that did little to endear him to his new wife. Estranged from Berenice, Antiochus returned to Laodice, who is strongly suspected to have poisoned her errant husband before he could change his mind once more.

On the death of Antiochus, Laodice quickly proclaimed her son by her late husband to be King Seleucus II, while just as quickly her supporters in Antioch murdered Berenice and her young child. Immediately after the succession, the Seleucid empire braced itself for the inevitable invasion by King Ptolemy, who was outraged by the death of his sister. The fraying of the Seleucid empire continued. Ptolemy was successful in his invasion and seized Syria, along with most of the Seleucid empire's other Mediterranean possessions and much of the east as well. Fortunately for Seleucus, Ptolemy had problems of his own back in Egypt, and these eventually forced him and his army to withdraw to his own domains.

The unorthodox manner by which Seleucus II had come to power had also alienated loyalists of the late murdered king, Antiochus II. Consequently a large faction of the nobility threw their support behind a younger son of the dead king, a youth also known as Antiochus, who gained the sobriquet Heirax (Hawk) because of his grasping and predatory nature.

It took considerable effort, but Seleucus II regained control of much of Syria. Thereafter he turned to Asia Minor, where his rebel brother and several different breakaway kingdoms needed his attention. On being defeated by his brother (at the Battle of Ancyra in 235 BC), Seleucus tried his luck at conquering the Parthians, but with his usual lack of success. Perhaps fortunately for his empire, he died in 225 BC after a fall from his horse. His son ruled for two years as Seleucus III. His reign was mostly taken up by wars in Anatolia, where he campaigned with such ineptitude that he was murdered by his exasperated army officers.

This brought to power a younger son of Seleucus II, the extraordinary Antiochus III, whose revitalization of the empire was to earn him the sobriquet 'the Great'. Under him the Seleucid empire was to reach its peak of power before an abrupt reversal of fortune inflicted by the legions of Rome.

Seleucid culture

The Seleucid empire was often viewed through Western eyes as a 'failed' attempt by the Greeks to Hellenize most of the Middle East. This perspective was strongly influenced by the contemporary opinion of the role of Western colonialism elsewhere in the world. Later twentieth-century historians have shown that the spread of Hellenic culture was largely unintended.

Certainly the Seleucid kings were keen promoters of Hellenism, but this was less for ideological reasons than because they saw the Greek language and culture as a common factor by which they could bring together peoples of otherwise very different traditions. Where it helped for them to adopt the local culture instead (as in Mesopotamia), this was done by the Seleucid kings just as enthusiastically as they promoted their own culture elsewhere. From the beginning, as Seleucus Nicator demonstrated by his marriage to a Sogdianan princess called Apame, the aim was a fusion of Greek and Eastern cultures rather than the suppression of one by the other.

This lack of a Hellenistic ideology was most apparent in warfare, a brutally Darwinist field where (as the Spartans had earlier discovered) the most effective techniques rapidly made obsolete the sentimental and political Greek fondness for traditional styles of warfare. The Seleucids retained the classical Macedonian phalanx – a solid block of men armed with pikes so long that the pikes of the second and third ranks could also engage the enemy. However, they made the pikes of the infantrymen somewhat longer, and supplemented the phalanx with very un-Macedonian scythed chariots and war elephants. Furthermore, many of the peoples of the Seleucid empire were skilled cavalrymen. Instead of forcing recruits from such nations into the phalanx, the Seleucids gave them the freedom to fight in their traditional fashion. This added to the Seleucid army light horsemen for scouting, horse archers for skirmishing and police work, and later the heavily armoured cavalry known as cataphracts – the nearest thing to a tank on an ancient battlefield. All these types of cavalry were largely absent from the army of Alexander.

The core of the army remained the phalanx, especially an elite core of phalangites known as the 'Silver Shields', but there are indications that membership of that unit was open to anyone with the right physical and social connections, regardless of ethnicity. By and large, apart from cavalry auxiliaries, the Hellenistic empires did little recruiting of local peoples, preferring to rely on Greek and Macedonian levies from immigrants in the new cities that they tirelessly founded.

As did the Ptolemies, the Seleucids maintained a mutant form of the early feudal system practised by the Persians. Soldiers, especially phalangites, were given tracts of farmland on which to settle when they were not on active service. This had the dual advantage of allowing the army to support itself when not needed, and making the soldiers well aware that they depended on the king for their farms; they therefore tended to give him their unswerving support. Many veterans were deliberately settled in potential trouble spots, and sometimes these military colonies were supplemented by fortresses manned by soldiers on active duty. The kings also built castles to guard strategic passes, trade routes and river crossings. Many of these, such as Dura-europos, became the nuclei of substantial cities in their own right.

Apart from such semi-spontaneous urban centres, the Seleucids deliberately founded hundreds of new cities across their domains. This was again mainly for the very practical reason that cities were useful economic and administrative centres. Certainly the kings promoted Hellenism in these cities, but mainly because the waves of immigrants they encouraged to settle from the Greek mainland would not have had it any other way.

However, no attempt was made to change traditions embedded in the local culture in regions where the new cities were located. A later exception to this near-universal tolerance was Judaism, but this was owing less to cultural imperialism on the part of the Seleucids and more to stubborn recidivism on the part of the Jews. Jewish culture and religion was the motive force behind the continued resistance of the Jewish people to Seleucid rule. If the Seleucids wanted Judaism stamped out it was not because they had anything against the underlying religion and culture, but because they saw

Statue of Artemis, a major contemporary goddess in Asia Minor, especially in Ephesus. The objects on her chest represent fertility, and are probably gourds. Classical copy of a geometric-era design.

The witch-goddess Hecate was worshipped at crossroads. The ancient 'crossroad' was what today we call a T-junction, so an interesting bit of trivia is that Hecate's Roman name was Trivia (Tri-via).

that without Judaism the Jews were more likely to stop rebelling. Where a cultural tradition happily accepted Seleucid overlordship – as did that of the Babylonians – the Seleucid kings not only allowed it to survive, but actively embraced and encouraged it.

One reason why Judaism refused to accept the Seleucids was because the rigidly monotheistic Jews were strongly opposed to the Seleucid presentation of themselves as divine or semi-divine beings who were under the special protection of the 'pagan' god Apollo. (It is usually Apollo who appears on the reverse of contemporary Seleucid coins.) As we have seen, the kings themselves were not based in a particular 'royal' city, but practised a very hands-on form of monarchy. Both the king and his court were constantly on the move, partly because the military situation demanded it and partly because regular visits by the king were a practical measure for maintaining his rule. Kings also kept up relations with cities off their regular itineraries through patronage, ruler cults and special privileges granted through the direct benevolence of the ruler. A king might also bestow deserving cities with temples or other civic buildings, and royal beneficence to loyal cities was expected in the event of natural disasters such as floods or earthquakes. For example, one of the last acts of Seleucus II before his riding accident was to send ships laden with corn and timber to the island city of Rhodes in the Mediterranean after a disastrous earthquake there.

Where the king did not rule directly (the kings spent most of their time in Syria, and visited Iran when possible), he assigned satrapies to his 'friends' – sometimes deserving Macedonian courtiers and ex-generals, but at other times, if suitably trustworthy candidates could be found, native sons of the region being governed. (It was a misjudgement of the trustworthiness of an Iranian aristocrat called Andragoras that led to the rebellion of the Parni and the foundation of the Parthian empire in 247 BC.) Below the satrap level there was little standardization of government, because the diversity of the empire made this impractical to impose. Where cities existed or were newly founded, they were made responsible for administration of their *chora* (a term roughly meaning 'rural hinterland'). In other areas, the local aristocrats were left to run things as they had been doing for centuries before the arrival of Alexander and the Greeks.

FIVE
MACEDON AND EGYPT

Because the conquerors of the east were Macedonians, it would be logical, but incorrect, to assume that Macedon itself was the most powerful of the kingdoms of the Hellenic era. In fact this was far from the case. Although never quite a backwater, Macedon never equalled the Seleucid or Ptolemaic kingdoms in either intellectual achievement or military power. Furthermore, far from showing great respect for the 'motherland', the Seleucids and Ptolemies regarded the Macedonian kingdom as just another player in the game for power and territorial advantage which – along with dynastic infighting – was their constant preoccupation.

Socially, Macedon was something of an outlier, retaining the earlier form of the kingship long abandoned by Greeks to the south. Yet at the same time the Macedonian kings were more down-to-earth than their more recent counterparts. The traditional aristocracy continued to play a considerable role in Macedonian politics and administration, and its members felt they had the right to be consulted before the king made any major decisions. While the common people of the eastern kingdoms were accustomed to their rulers demanding worship as gods (indeed, in some cases the demand came from the common people who wanted to worship their rulers as such), the Macedonians were firmly convinced that their rulers were human. As with their eastern counterparts, Macedonian kings had the dubious privilege of being polygamous, not least because multiple wives made the creation of diplomatic marriage alliances a lot easier.

Another way in which Macedon was unique among the Hellenistic kingdoms was that it was the era's only real nation-state. Macedon was a nation of Macedonians ruled by a Macedonian. Compare this with the Greeks further south who were divided into hundreds of competing polities; or with Egypt, where the northern cities were an uneasy fusion of native, Greek and Semitic cultures, and the race and culture of the rulers were very different from those living in the heartland of the country. The Seleucid empire represented not one nation or people but dozens, all of whom had very little in common apart from their ruler, and that ruler belonged to none of the native peoples of that empire. In short, Macedon was an integrated state in a way that no others were, including the nascent power of contemporary Rome.

In part this unity was forced upon the Macedonian people as a result of their geographical circumstances. The core of Macedon was the southern region – a fertile plain between the Haliakmon and Axius rivers – but in the generations before Philip ii the Macedonians had expanded northwards and westwards, taking in dozens of formerly independent tribes in the process. Except where it bordered on the Aegean Sea, Macedon's natural boundaries were mountain ranges, such as the Olympos range, which separated the kingdom from the rest of Greece, and the Rhodope range, which separated Macedon from Thrace to the east.

The Macedonian perception that theirs was a relatively small kingdom surrounded by enemies was not entirely untrue. To the south was the Greek peninsula, the cities of which had been subjugated to Macedon since the time of Philip ii, and it would be fair to say that few of those cities were happy about it. To the southwest was the kingdom of Epirus, a powerful federal state that was, fortunately for Macedon, generally too preoccupied with internal politics to take advantage of temporary Macedonian weakness.

This weakness was often caused by the necessity of bringing troops north and east to fight off barbarian incursions that periodically – as with the Galatians in the 280s BC – escalated to become full-scale invasions. It was a common Macedonian complaint that the Greeks to the south were free to indulge in their inter-city squabbles and disunity because Macedon to the north bore the

Inside of a bowl depicting a woman with the dress and hairstyle of the Hellenistic era. Date unknown.

brunt of barbarian attacks alone, unthanked and unaided. In fact, when the southern Greeks of the fifth century BC deigned to notice the Macedonians at all it was to sneer at them for being uncouth and backward.

Nevertheless the Macedonians were far from being passive victims, as the Thracians could testify. The mineral-rich lands to their east constantly tempted the Macedonian kings to seek out and seize Thracian territory, which they exploited to their advantage, and everyone agreed very early on that the Macedonians were tough, stubborn fighters.

Political history

The history of Macedon as a fully unified nation-state began in the early fourth century under Amyntas III, who led the northern expansion fifty years or so after the state emerged from a period of vassalage to the Persian empire. This northern expansion might have happened earlier had the Macedonians not been preoccupied with fending off the predatory advances of the Athenians, who, like the Macedonians, coveted the rich resources of Thrace. Only once Athens had been comprehensively defeated in the Peloponnesian War (431–404 BC) were the Macedonians free to pursue their northern agenda.

The additional manpower and resources that the unified state gave its kings provided the impetus for Philip II to expand into Thrace later and then to dominate southern Greece. Philip's son Alexander then used the Macedonian army to conquer Persia and create the Hellenistic world of the east. However, Macedon itself derived little benefit from this expansion. For a start, the military manpower of the state was drained to feed Alexander's armies. Even after they had served their time, most soldiers did not return home to Macedon, being instead settled (with varying degrees of reluctance) as military colonists in Alexander's new domains. A host of artisanal talent from metalworkers to coiners to farriers followed the soldiers to support the army and later to profit from business opportunities in the newly conquered lands. Many traders and merchantmen left both Macedonia and Greece for the same reason, stripping their homelands of talented innovators and craftsmen.

Thereafter, the rise of the Seleucid and Ptolemaic empires made the new eastern kingdoms not allies but rivals, and as much a threat to Macedonian autonomy as the Persian empire had once been. The Seleucids, especially under the early monarchs, were a direct threat to Macedonian sovereignty, as Seleucus Nicator proved by his attempted invasion in 281 BC. The influence of the Ptolemies was more indirect but equally malign. The Ptolemaic kings were very interested in expanding their domains into the Mediterranean via Crete and Cyprus, and on different occasions attempted to bribe Greek city-states into switching their allegiance. Athens was a natural target, because of its strong naval tradition. Also, the state had possessed a natural antipathy to Macedon since the time of Philip II, whom the Athenian orator Demosthenes described as

> not a Greek, nor even a relative of the Greeks. Even as a barbarian he does not come from any place that can be described as distinguished. He is a poxy scumbag from Macedonia, a place where one cannot even buy a decent slave. (*Third Philippic*, 31)

The Athenians rebelled against Macedon on the death of Philip II in 336 BC, again in the Lamian War of 323 BC, again in the Chremonidian War of 268–262 BC (with Ptolemy II actively pitching in against the Macedonians on this occasion), and again in 224 BC. Nor were the Athenians alone in their insubordinate attitude toward their Macedonian overlords. Other Greek states, either singly or in confederations, periodically attempted to assert their independence, forcing the Macedonian kings to bring their armies south whenever they could spare the time from fighting off barbarian raids on their northern and eastern frontiers.

The Antigonid dynasty

After Alexander's death, Macedon was ruled briefly by Antipater, the general sent by Perdiccas to take charge of Greece and Macedon as a viceroy for Alexander's children. On his deathbed in 319 BC Antipater tried to avoid passing the regency to his son, the unscrupulous and ambitious Cassander, but Cassander took it anyway. The new 'regent' spent the early years of his reign assassinating, poisoning and executing as many of Alexander's kin as he felt might have a claim to the throne, and added Alexander's wife, Roxane, and mother, Olympias, to the list, both to forestall their support for any claimant and to prevent the involvement of Olympias in politics. By 305 BC Cassander was secure enough in Macedon to declare himself king, a title he enjoyed for eight years before he died of natural causes. Thereafter his family tore itself apart in dynastic infighting, leaving the way to the succession clear for the Antigonid dynasty.

The Antigonids were of the family of Antigonus the One-eyed, whose son Demetrios briefly seized the Macedonian throne during one of the more successful moments in his chequered career. The son of Demetrios was Antigonus Gonatas (277–239 BC), who gave the dynasty credibility by restoring the state from a period of near-anarchy. His first military success was in repelling an army of Celtic invaders from Macedon in 276 BC. Thereafter he faced down Ptolemaic and Epirot interventions in southern Greece and re-established the Macedonian primacy there. Though a competent general, Antigonus Gonatas preferred to husband his military resources and achieve his aims through diplomacy, at which he

Bas-relief of a contemporary merchant vessel. Such ships traded around the
Mediterranean with little regard to the political boundaries of the time, since trade
was encouraged by rulers of all stripes.

was equally skilled. He managed to establish Macedonian naval
supremacy in the Aegean, but tireless plotting by the Ptolemies
had weakened the Macedonian grip on southern Greece by the
time he died in 239 BC at the age of eighty.

The Stoic philosopher Zeno was one of the guiding influences
of Antigonus' career, causing that monarch to regard his kingship as one of 'noble servitude' to the people over whom he ruled.
Unusually for a Hellenistic monarch, Antigonus was on good
terms with his son, another Demetrios. In fact, Antigonus trusted
his son enough to allow him to lead an army against Epirus, and
it seems probable that by the time of Antigonus' death Demetrios
was already virtually his co-ruler. Once Demetrios had become
sole ruler as Demetrios II of Macedon, military affairs took most
of his attention. After ten years fighting the Epirots (who were

Though damaged, this bust shows the exceptional skill and artistry of Alexandrian sculptors working in the Classical Greek tradition.

going through a period of military expansionism and political turmoil), and repelling incursions by the Illyrians and the Aetolians, Demetrios was finally defeated in a battle against invading Dardanian tribesmen, and died soon thereafter.

The son of Demetrios was too young to assume the monarchy. Instead, a relative called Antigonus Doson stepped up to serve as regent. He made a competent start in this role by expelling the Dardanians who had accounted for his predecessor, and suppressing a revolt that broke out in Thessaly following the news of Demetrios' death. Thereafter, with the enthusiastic support of the army, Doson finessed his regency into a monarchy, becoming King Antigonus III of Macedon. In the usual way of Macedonian dynastic politics this would have meant the death of Demetrios' young son, but despite taking the kingship from the boy, Doson not only left the lad unharmed but made him his heir.

As king, Doson also had little time for other than military matters, partly thanks to the ambitions of Cleomenes III of Sparta, who had dreams of restoring his city's dominance of the Peloponnese. With the diplomatic skills that were a hallmark of the Antigonid dynasty, Doson fashioned an alliance of Greek states that overwhelmed the Spartans at the Battle of Sellasia in 222 BC. Then, while the dust was still settling in Greece, Doson had to rush north with his army to deal with another Illyrian invasion of Macedon. Yet again Doson was victorious, but the battle cost him his life, leaving the succession to Demetrios' son, who now took the throne as Philip V.

Rather like his contemporary Antiochus III of Syria, Philip was an exceptional ruler. He and Antiochus might together have raised the Hellenistic kingdoms to new heights, had not both kings been defeated and crippled by the rising power of Rome.

Ptolemaic Egypt

On Alexander's death, the decision of his general Ptolemy to seize Egypt and hold that kingdom and that kingdom alone must have seemed puzzling to his contemporaries. Egypt would not have been the first choice of any of the other successor generals, even if Ptolemy had given them the chance. The kingdom was isolated from the rest of the Mediterranean world by desert and sea, and offered little chance of expansion. The grim and continual resistance offered by the Egyptians to their Persian conquerors suggested that a people proud of their tradition of thousands of years of independence would not submit readily to a foreign overlord. Yet not only did Ptolemy claim Egypt as his kingdom, but he spurned the opportunity to take over other possessions in order to consolidate his rule there. The result was arguably the most successful and brilliant of all the Hellenistic kingdoms, transplanted into what seemed at first to be the most unpromising soil.

Egyptian history in the Ptolemaic period is made all the more confusing by the fact that every one of its kings was called Ptolemy. (The line finished with Ptolemy xv, also known as Caesarion after his father, Julius Caesar.) To make things even more complex, the Ptolemies were in the habit of marrying their closest female relatives, be these sisters, cousins or aunts. These females were invariably called Berenice (the bearer of Nike, 'victory'), Arsinoe or Cleopatra. Thus the Cleopatra who was mother to Ptolemy xv was the widow of her husband-brother Ptolemy xiv and the seventh Egyptian Cleopatra to bear that name.

The Ptolemaic subjects were undisturbed by the highly incestuous nature of their royal family: the Greeks because their kings proclaimed themselves divine, and incest was common enough among Greek gods (even Zeus, king of the gods, was married to his sister Hera); the Egyptians because their pharaohs had allegedly indulged in similar practices for centuries (whether they actually did is now uncertain). Nor did this energetic inbreeding appear to do particular harm to the line – Cleopatra vii seduced Mark Antony as much by her charm and brilliant mind as by her looks, which the historian Plutarch describes as average at best.

While brother–sister marriage did no harm to the reputation of the Ptolemies as rulers of Egypt, what caused them to be accepted by the native population was the manner in which they presented themselves to the Egyptians as traditional pharaohs. It turned out that the native Egyptians minded less that their pharaohs were foreign than that they resided in Egypt and behaved (at least in public) as traditional monarchs. Art and sculpture depicting the Ptolemies in Egypt shows the rulers in traditional Egyptian royal regalia paying proper deference to the gods of Egypt. Consequently, while much is rightly made of the Hellenistic flowering of Greek thought in Alexandria, Cyrene and 'Greek' cities in Ptolemaic Egypt, Egyptian culture enjoyed a minor renaissance of its own. Many of the

Egyptian temples visited by modern tourists, such as those at Philae, Edfu and Dendra, are largely Ptolemaic.

PTOLEMY I

The mother of the first Ptolemy of Egypt was called Arsinoe. In his later propaganda Ptolemy claimed Philip II as his father, making him a half-brother of Alexander by posthumous self-adoption. This claim obscures whom the actual father might have been, though sceptical ancient historians rejected Ptolemy's claim of Philip II in favour of Lagus, an obscure Macedonian nobleman.

Ptolemy was one of Alexander's childhood friends, and later one of his most trusted generals. Perdiccas, the regent who took power after the death of Alexander, also trusted Ptolemy, but as we have seen, when sent to campaign against the rebel satrap Cleomenes in Egypt, Ptolemy simply took Cleomenes' place and added insult to injury by hijacking Alexander's corpse and installing it with all reverence in Alexandria. Though he gave lip service to the successors of Alexander, in reality Ptolemy was his own man and everybody knew it.

This was formalized several wars later, when further dynastic struggles led to the extirpation of the line of Alexander the Great. Ptolemy followed the example of the former regent Antigonus the One-eyed, who declared himself king. As we have seen, Ptolemy and the other successor generals (now kings) thereafter joined forces to overthrow Antigonus.

Secure behind Egypt's natural defences, Ptolemy sat out many of the successor wars of the 280s BC. Already Egypt's new ruler was taking an interest in matters academic and was contemplating the projects that later became the famed Museum and Library of Alexandria. Ptolemy had also married a woman called Berenice (naturally) and had a son by her, inevitably also named Ptolemy.

PTOLEMY II

This Ptolemy is distinguished from his father by his sobriquet 'Philadelphos'. (The first Ptolemy is sometimes known as Ptolemy ı Soter – the Saviour – though whom or what he saved is unclear.) The 'brotherly love' implied by the name Philadelphos was not extended to Ptolemy ıı's elder brother, who left Egypt when it became clear that he would not inherit the throne. However, this love was certainly extended to Ptolemy's sister Arsinoe ıı, whom he married after he repudiated his first wife, Arsinoe ı, who was the daughter of the king of Macedon and the mother of his

Ptolemy ıı of Egypt, as depicted on a gold octodrachm, *c.* 272 BC.

successor, Ptolemy III. As well as with his sister, Ptolemy enjoyed liaisons with a vast number of concubines and courtesans, giving his court a well-deserved reputation for moral decadence.

Known to the Egyptians as 'the mighty son of Ra, the beloved of Amon', this ruler was presented in Egyptian statuary in a typical pharaoh's headdress and clothing. This acceptance of Egyptian religion and tradition did much to make Ptolemy II acceptable to his Egyptian subjects, although their new pharaoh had actually been born on the Greek island of Cos.

As might be expected of the child of an academically minded father, Ptolemy II's education was assigned to the best tutors available in his day. Consequently, while his personal life was renowned for its dissolution and excess, the intellectual achievements of Egypt during his reign were even more remarkable. It was under Ptolemy II that Alexandria become the foremost destination for the leading poets, philosophers, sculptors and artists of the day. Many of the leading thinkers of the Hellenistic world were attracted to the new Library, which was founded by Ptolemy I but came to its full potential under his son. In fact the Library, with its reading rooms, scroll depositories and dining room, was only part of the larger building complex in which it was housed. This included a zoo, dissecting rooms and an observatory, as well as facilities for meetings, seminars and lectures. Indeed, although lacking a student body, the institution had many of the facilities recognizable in a modern university, including positions for tenured staff, research fellows and visiting professors. Rather as modern places of study are known as 'academies' after the Academy in Athens where Plato taught, so modern institutions are known as 'museums' after the Museum, or Temple to the Muses, near which Ptolemy's original library and research institution was founded.

Even sports benefited from royal patronage. As we have seen, all Greeks, including those from the far-flung colonies across the Mediterranean and beyond, were able to participate in the Olympic Games, as now did all Macedonians, since the masters of Delphi and Greece insisted that Macedonians were as Greek as any of their southern counterparts. The celebration of their common culture at the Games did much to solidify the Greek concept of themselves as a single people, whether they dwelt in Baetica (in modern Spain) or Bactria (in modern Uzbekistan).

Noting the success of the Olympics as a pan-Hellenic festival, Ptolemy III instituted games named after his line, the Ptolemaieia. These were held every four years, and came to rival the Olympics in the quality of the athletes who attended.

Alexandria was not just a university city. The care taken by Alexander's city planners was evident not only in minor details, such as the way the streets were laid out to get maximum benefit from the prevailing winds, but in the location of the city itself. It rapidly became the gateway between Egypt and the rest of the Mediterranean world (which had an insatiable appetite for ivory and papyrus, especially since the latter could not be made to flourish anywhere else). Yet the ambition of the Ptolemies went much further than this. As a general of Alexander, Ptolemy I had seen how the fabulous Silk Road brought wealth to those living along the route, and he was determined to appropriate some of that wealth for his new kingdom. Consequently, Ptolemy II is known to have actively courted the kings of India (for example, the later Roman encyclopaedist Pliny the Elder tells us that the writer Dionysius was sent to live with an Indian king with the express purpose of improving relations – including trade – between that kingdom and Egypt (*Natural History* 21)). This proved a far-sighted step, since the monsoon trade winds were more than capable of bearing ships loaded with exotic cargoes to Red Sea ports for the brief overland portage to Alexandria and dissemination from there throughout the Mediterranean world. (Ptolemy is believed to have introduced the camel – previously barely known in Egypt – for this purpose.)

For the rest of antiquity the Silk Road took a southward fork in central Asia, with many merchants preferring to sell goods south through India, and these went onwards to Europe via Alexandria. To further this trade Ptolemy also built a canal to the Red Sea from the Pelusiac branch of the Nile. This project had been considered by earlier rulers, but abandoned when it was discovered that the Red Sea and the Nile were at different levels. Since the Red Sea was higher there was a real risk of a saltwater flood. Ptolemy harnessed the intellectual energy of his age to come up with the solution – a series of locks not much different in principle from those still used today on the Suez canal.

Ptolemy II used his nation's wealth to further invest in a Mediterranean fleet and dominance of the Aegean trade routes. Egypt consequently flourished economically as much as intellectually, and this wealth paid for an army of mercenaries. Ptolemy may have been an intellectual, but he still had the preoccupation that his family shared with their fellow Hellenistic monarchs – warfare.

While sharing a common culture, the Greeks had never let that stop them from taking every opportunity to weaken and discomfit their neighbours, even when those neighbours were as Hellenic as themselves. Likewise Ptolemy felt little solidarity with his fellow Hellenistic rulers, and would (for example) happily support an Athenian rebellion against Macedon or stage an opportunistic land grab in the Levant while the Seleucids were engaged in an internecine dynastic feud. Unlike his Macedonian and Seleucid counterparts, Ptolemy II had little inclination for leading armies personally, and such was the repute of his dynasty that he seems to have had little fear of disloyalty among his generals.

Ptolemy's reign was not altogether free from intrigue, since it was palace plots that led to the downfall and exile of his first wife and her replacement by his sister-bride. It is less certain whether the actual plotting was done by the first wife against Ptolemy, or whether this wife was set up by Ptolemy's sister, who was not only beautiful and accomplished but a consummate and ruthless politician. Certainly, once she was in power Arsinoe II was an advisor and confidante of her brother and husband. She also adopted the children of his previous marriage, and it was one of these who succeeded to power on Ptolemy II's death in 246 BC.

PTOLEMY III EUERGETES 'THE BENEFACTOR'

The four themes of this Ptolemy's rule all built on the strengths of the kingdom established by his predecessors. These were the encouragement of intellectual accomplishment, the development of trade, integration with the Egyptian priestly establishment, and causing as much trouble as possible for his fellow Hellenistic kings.

The ruins of this Ptolemaic-era temple on the island of Philae on the Nile show clear cross-cultural influence.

Admittedly, Ptolemy had more of an incentive than most to go after the Seleucid kingdom. As described earlier, he married his sister Berenice in good faith to the Seleucid king Antiochus II, only for the unfortunate woman to be assassinated by that ruler's ambitious ex-wife. As soon as he came to power, the vindictive Ptolemy invaded and took large amounts of the Seleucid kingdom by way of compensation. While he was away from Egypt he left the state under the control of his wife (another Berenice). Unrest at his absence forced him to return to take control once again, though his hasty departure from Syria meant that he was unable to consolidate his gains there. There are indications that the trouble in Egypt was partly instigated by Antigonus II Gonatas of Macedon, and an ill-recorded naval battle near the island of Andros resulted from the consequent dip in already poor Egypto-Macedonian relations.

Ptolemy III worked hard to consolidate his dynasty's position with the Egyptian people, and began work on several temples to the Egyptian gods at Edfu, Karnak and elsewhere. A welcome incidental benefit of the Syrian campaign was that his armies advanced as far as Babylon, and in the process retrieved and returned to Egypt statues and other sacred objects looted by the Persians during their period of occupation.

The famous Library continued to go from strength to strength. Ptolemy had ships arriving in Alexandria searched for useful texts, and if any were found, they were confiscated and the owners compensated with copies made by the Library's scribes. Ptolemy also asked the Athenians for the original versions of the works of Euripides, Aeschylus and Sophocles, saying that they were needed to correct the copies held by the Library. He gave the Athenians a fabulously large deposit for the safe return of the works and then reneged on the deal, making this one of the only cases in history where it was the Library that paid a fine for not returning books. The fact that Ptolemy could sacrifice almost the equivalent of a year's tribute from Judaea for these venerated works was a deliberate display of his kingdom's wealth, and a reflection of how determined the Ptolemies were to make Egypt a centre of Hellenic culture.

Beacon of Hellenism

All the early Ptolemies worked hard to develop Alexandria's potential as a trading port. To this end Ptolemy I Soter had ordered his engineers to start work on a lighthouse on the island of Pharos near the harbour mouth. Typically, Ptolemy thought not of a mundane lighthouse, but of something on an epic scale. So epic was the construction, in fact, that the tower was not finished in his lifetime but was brought to completion by his son.

The Roman writer Lucian adds an interesting tale of how the credit for this work was claimed:

> That great architect from Cnidus [a Greek city in Asia Minor] was the builder of the Pharos tower, a building without compare for size and beauty . . . When construction was done, he engraved on the stone his own name. Then he covered the inscription with plaster on which he dedicated the building

to the reigning king. As he intended, in later years the plaster and dedication eventually fell away, leaving the words

Sostratus, son of Dexiphanes of Cnidus
[built this] on behalf of all sailors
[and dedicates it] to the saviour gods (*Sacred Texts*, 62)

Credit was well worth claiming. The lighthouse was acclaimed right from the start as one of the architectural wonders of the age, and it endured through all of antiquity before being destroyed by a series of earthquakes in the Middle Ages. While it is often depicted on coins and mentioned in texts, some of the best descriptions come from Arab scholars who saw the lighthouse after it had been partially destroyed. From their description and from surviving depictions of the building, it appears that the lighthouse had a high rectangular base with a conical tower built upon that.

The interval between base and tower was already high enough to serve as a viewing platform, and ancient texts speak of meals being served to tourists there. Overall, base and tower made an edifice at least 120 metres tall, just 30 metres under the height that modern architecture specifies for designating a building as a 'sky-scraper'. This means that the lighthouse was the size of a thirty-storey building, and the stone blocks at the base had to be held together with 'mortar' of molten lead so as to withstand the pounding of the waves. (These blocks survive as underwater remains, and are substantial pieces of stonework weighing between 50 and 75 tons each.)

By day the lighthouse was by itself enough to serve as a navigational aid even for sailors far out to sea. It could be seen up to 175 kilometres away, because even if the lighthouse itself was not visible, the smoke from the fire at the top extended in a column at least as high again as the actual building. By some (probably fanciful) accounts, the light from this fire was amplified at night by specially moulded glass windows.

From the point of view of the Ptolemaic kings, the lighthouse was a great success. Not only did it literally broadcast the power and wealth of Egypt, but it did so in a functional manner that ingrained this work of propaganda into the infrastructure and imagination of the ancient Mediterranean world. Even today, in many languages (French, Spanish and Greek, for example) the word for 'lighthouse' is a derivative of the word 'Pharos'.

Eratosthenes

Another example of the extraordinary intellectual flowering of Hellenistic thought in Egypt is the career of the mathematician and poet Eratosthenes of Cyrene, chief librarian of the Library of Alexandria under Ptolemy III. Perhaps the most extraordinary of his achievements were both to calculate the axial tilt of the Earth and to make a remarkably good estimate of its size.

The Greeks of Eratosthenes' day knew that the Earth was a sphere, for the very good reason that they saw its shadow on the moon every eclipse. To calculate the size of that sphere, Eratosthenes made the heroic assumption that the sun was so far

Drawing of the Pharos of Alexandria by the German archaeologist Professor H. Thiersch, 1909.

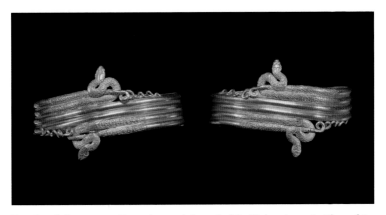

Bracelets fit for a queen. Created toward the end of the Ptolemaic era in Alexandria, jewellery such as this was certainly worn by Cleopatra.

away that for all practical purposes its rays were parallel wherever they struck the planet. (This assumption was by no means a given at the time.) Therefore, he reasoned, the sun's rays would strike the Earth at different angles depending on where one was standing on the sphere. By calculating these angles at Alexandria and at Cyrene, 5,000 stades (a unit of length) to the south, Eratosthenes worked out that the difference was just over 7 degrees. Since a circle is 360 degrees, the 5,000 stadions to Syene were one-fiftieth of the planet's circumference.

Actually, since the Earth is not a perfect sphere, and because Cyrene and Alexandria were not on exactly the same meridian, Eratosthenes failed to produce an exact measurement. The margin of error was between 10 and 16 per cent depending on which measurement of a stade he used (the original measurement of 180 metres per stade is where we get the modern word 'stadium', but there were several variations on the stade in the ancient world, just as a gallon is different in the USA and UK today).

Nevertheless, the estimate of Eratosthenes was better than any before the modern era. If Christopher Columbus in 1492 had followed Eratosthenes instead of relying on his own heroically incorrect calculations, he would never have tried to reach India by sailing westwards from Iberia. As it was, he thought he had reached his destination when he accidentally discovered the Americas less than halfway through the actual journey.

The Syrian Wars: a summary to 241 BC

Between 301 and 150 BC Ptolemaic Egypt and the Seleucid east were in a constant state of tension that regularly flared up into war. These have been referred to as they happened, but the so-called Syrian Wars are so much a part of the history of the time that they merit a formal description in their own right. The table below serves as a quick reference to the first and most important three of the overall six. (The final three wars were minor and complex affairs which only hastened the fall of the Seleucid kingdom.)

The First Syrian War
Dates: 274–271 BC
Protagonists: Ptolemy II and the Galatians vs Antiochus I
Casus belli: Egyptian interference to prevent Seleucid expansion in Anatolia
Significant battles: Antiochus defeats the Galatians in the Battle of the Elephants, 275 BC
Territorial changes: Egypt makes gains around Caria and Cilicia, but temporarily loses Cyrenaica in Africa to a usurper
Overall result: Ptolemaic win

The Second Syrian War
Dates: 260–253 BC
Protagonists: Ptolemy II vs Antiochus II and Antigonus Gonatas
Casus belli: The Seleucids combine forces with Macedon to push back Ptolemaic gains
Significant battles: Macedon defeats the Egyptian fleet at the Battle of Cos in 258 BC
Territorial changes: Seleucid gains in Asia Minor, loss of Ptolemaic power in the Aegean
Overall result: Ptolemaic loss

The Third Syrian War

Dates: 246–241 BC

Protagonists: Ptolemy III vs Seleucus II and Antigonus Gonatas

Casus belli: The murder of Berenice, the Egyptian woman married to Antiochus as part of the settlement of the Second Syrian War

Significant battles: Macedon defeats the Egyptian fleet at the Battle of Andros

Territorial changes: Ptolemaic gains in Asia Minor, loss of the Cyclades Islands to Antigonus

Overall result: Ptolemaic win

SIX

ROME AND THE HELLENISTIC KINGDOMS

W hile the intellectual life of the Romans benefitted greatly from interaction with the Hellenic states, this did not stop the Romans from using their military power to defeat and destroy the Hellenistic kingdoms. What might have become of these kingdoms without Roman intervention is one of the fascinating 'what ifs?' of history.

Macedon

With the fall of Syracuse, Rome's hold on Sicily was secure. As Pyrrhus had suggested, the Romans then took the next logical step and went on to invade and conquer Carthage, thus forcing the surrender of Hannibal and the end of the Second Punic War (218–202 BC). Next was the Greek mainland and Macedonia.

The Romans had an excuse for involving themselves in the affairs of Greece because in 215 BC, after Rome's catastrophic defeat by Hannibal at Cannae, Philip v of Macedon had declared war on Rome. Ever since the time of Pyrrhus it had been a Roman nightmare that the Hellenistic kingdoms with their far greater wealth and resources would turn on Rome. In reality Philip had little interest in getting involved in an Italian war. He had declared war on Rome only because his proposed ally, Hannibal, was already fighting the Romans. However, the Romans did not realize this. They were, nevertheless, well aware that their defeat of Pyrrhus and Hannibal had brought them to the notice of the Hellenistic powers, and that this new-found attention was unlikely to be friendly.

Therefore, with the west secure, the Romans were intent on getting their retaliation in first. Though a temporary peace had been patched up with Macedon while the Romans had their hands full with Hannibal, when the time was right the Romans had always intended to repay what they saw as the treachery of Philip v.

Accordingly the ink was barely dry on the terms of Carthage's surrender when, in 200 BC, Rome declared war. This war is known as the Second Macedonian War, of 200–196 BC. (The First Macedonian War had consisted of desultory fighting, mainly between Philip's allies and Rome's dependants in Illyria. For the second war, the Romans could bring to bear their full army of highly experienced veterans.)

The coming clash was awaited with deep interest by military observers throughout the Hellenistic world, where it was hotly debated whether the pikes of the Macedonian phalanx would overcome the *pilums* of the Roman legions. Certainly none of the Hellenistic kingdoms felt the slightest urge to come to Philip's aid against the 'barbarian' Romans. Philip had done little to endear himself to his fellow monarchs.

In Egypt Ptolemy III had died in 222 BC, and it quickly became apparent that the ministers who ruled for the boy-pharaoh Ptolemy IV were markedly incompetent. That was all the excuse the highly competent Antiochus III of the Seleucid empire needed to fall upon the lands in the Levant and Syria that previous Ptolemies had taken from his empire, and retake them for his own. (Antiochus would have done this even sooner, but he had spent much of his early reign consolidating his empire's eastern frontier.)

With Egypt weak and Antiochus preoccupied elsewhere, Philip busily began expanding Macedonian power into the Aegean, taking Ptolemaic bases and also capturing previously free cities such as the trading ports of Cius and Thasos. The subsequent disruption of Mediterranean trade brought Philip into conflict with the nascent kingdom of Pergamon in Asia Minor and the free city of Rhodes, but Macedonian naval power prevailed over both these rivals.

Nothing in what we see of Philip's activities prior to the Second Macedonian War shows that he had any interest in Rome or the west. Rather, he had all the standard preoccupations of a Macedonian king – keeping Greece under Macedonian hegemonic control, fending off barbarian attacks from the north, and preventing the more powerful kingdoms of Seleucia and Egypt from overwhelming his own. To Philip, the Romans were simply a more-than-usually organized barbarian distraction, and his main aim throughout the war was simply to make the Romans give up and go away. His stance was defensive, and we certainly see no plans to attack westwards in the manner in which Philip engaged with eastern cities. In fact, when the Romans declared war on him, Philip was engaged in the siege of one such city and paid scant attention to the Roman ambassador.

Neither were the Romans looking for territorial gains. Rather, their intention was to cripple Macedon to the point where that kingdom was no longer a threat to their nascent empire in the west. The Romans correctly divined that wresting Greece from Macedonian control was most likely to achieve their objective. Accordingly, the declared intent of the Roman invasion that followed the declaration of war was the ostensibly altruistic intention to 'free Greece'.

This claim was enough to convince the Athenians, who had never fully accepted Macedonian overlordship. Philip's former allies in the Aetolian League also took the Roman side, since they felt the king had treated them badly in the previous war. In the east Pergamon readily accepted an invitation to renew hostilities with Macedon, so it appeared that the Romans had successfully managed the diplomatic encirclement of their foe.

The problem, as the Romans swiftly discovered, was that encircling Macedon was one thing, but actually invading it was something else entirely. The natural mountain defences of the kingdom were formidable, and when they were reinforced by Philip's highly competent soldiery, even Roman veterans were unable to make much headway.

Philip then proposed very reasonable peace terms, again with the intention of finishing off a war he had never wanted. Given their disappointing progress with the war to date, the Romans might have accepted were it not that their commander in the field was the very ambitious Flamininus. Flamininus appealed to his friends

This view of the landscape of northern Greece shows the difficulties faced by Roman armies as they attempted to force an approach to Macedonia.

in the Roman senate to get his period of command extended for another year. If they could do that, his faction would endeavour to sabotage the peace proposal. If Flamininus were not given the extended command, his faction would vote for peace in order that Flamininus should at least have the kudos of having brought the war to a moderately successful end.

This sort of internal Roman politicking was to happen time and again during Rome's engagement with the Hellenistic east, and the abrupt policy shifts and backtracking that resulted from it caused the Hellenistic kings much exasperation and misunderstanding. Also, because Flamininus' lust for glory was more often than not shared by his contemporaries, it meant that sometimes the Hellenistic kings were unable to make peace on any terms. The need to appear before the electorate as conquering generals easily outweighed any diplomatic considerations in the minds of the Roman aristocracy.

The Romans appeared to be sincere in their desire to liberate Greece, and this, combined with the selective Roman destruction of cities that refused to be 'liberated', brought Greece almost entirely on to the Roman side. In 197 BC Flamininus was therefore able to bring his armies across Greece to Thessaly, the point at which Macedon was most approachable. Philip's army met the Romans at a place called Cynoscephalae – 'the Dog's Heads' – in a confused engagement in which the phalanx was unable to deploy to best advantage. The Roman victory forced Philip to accept Roman terms.

In 196 BC Flamininus proclaimed the liberty of the Greeks to an ecstatic crowd at the opening of the Isthmian Games in Corinth. Some of the more cynical in the crowd noted that while 'freeing' the Greeks, the Romans had placed their own garrisons in the fortresses at Corinth, Chalcis and Demetrias – strongpoints so strategic that they were known as the 'fetters of Greece'. There was also a hidden irony in the choice of Corinth for Flamininus' declaration. Almost exactly fifty years after they proclaimed Greece 'free', the Romans were to raze Corinth to the ground in the process of absorbing Greece into their empire.

Seleucia

Philip's problems were highly beneficial to Antiochus III of the Seleucids. With the Romans keeping Philip off his back, Antiochus was free to concentrate his entire attention on pushing the Egyptians south beyond Gaza. At the Battle of Panium in 201 BC, Antiochus destroyed the main Egyptian force in the region, and he spent the next three years removing the Ptolemaic presence from Syria and the southern Aegean. Antiochus was too strategically aware to risk attacking the natural defences of Egypt proper, so in 195 BC he consolidated his gains by making peace with Egypt. This left him free to consider his next move – taking advantage of Macedonian weakness by moving into Philip V's sphere of influence.

Certainly affairs in Greece looked ripe for Seleucid interference. As anyone who knew contemporary Greek politics might have guessed, it had not taken the Greeks long to become disillusioned with their Roman 'protectors'. The Spartans were eager to regain some of their lost military glory, and the Aetolians were angry with Rome because they felt they had been insufficiently rewarded for their role in the war against Macedon. Another confederation of Greek cities – the Achaeans – were eager to annex Sparta and put an end to that city's troublesome ways.

Therefore when the Aetolians attempted to seize the fortresses of Corinth, Chalcis and Demetrias and the Achaeans took Sparta, Antiochus decided that the situation was sufficiently chaotic for him to step in. In the autumn of 192 BC he invaded Greece under the tired old pretext that he was actually 'liberating' its peoples.

Antiochus might have expected resistance from Philip. He might also have expected the Romans to object to his intervention in their new protectorate. What he probably did not expect was that Philip would enthusiastically ally himself with his former enemies and that the Roman aristocracy would happily rush into a full-scale war in their pursuit of military glory. In this case Antiochus was opposed by a Roman parvenu who had already alienated many of his fellow Romans by his energetic attempts to restore old-fashioned morality to state affairs. This was Cato the Elder.

Despite his ostensible scorn for Greek culture, Cato knew his history. When Antiochus tried to make a stand at Thermopylae, just as Leonidas had made his epic stand against the Persians three hundred years previously, Cato defeated Antiochus just as the Persians had defeated Leonidas – by taking an outflanking force through the mountains. After this setback Antiochus accepted that his European adventure had failed, and withdrew to Asia Minor. It probably did not occur to him that the Romans might follow him even there, but they did.

The Romans worked together with their allies in the Anatolian city of Pergamum and first ensured local naval superiority. Then they crossed to Asia Minor with an army commanded by Lucius Scipio, brother of that Scipio Africanus who had been instrumental in the defeat of Hannibal in the Second Punic War. (Scipio Africanus was also with the army, though constitutionally prevented from taking command.) Hannibal himself was present as well, though on the other side. He was serving as an advisor to King Antiochus, having fled to the Seleucids once it became clear that the Romans would want his death if he remained in Carthage.

Hannibal had some success as an admiral fighting the fleet of the Rhodians (who were allied to Rome at this time). However, his role was peripheral to the main contest, which was decided on land at the Battle of Magnesia in 190 BC. Antiochus was successful in the part of the battle where he commanded personally, but the legions successfully defeated their opponents on the left wing. The Romans then used their superior manoeuvrability to hit the ponderous Seleucid pike phalanx in the flank and win a crushing victory. Like Philip before him, Antiochus was forced to terms, and was compelled not only to renounce all claims to Greece, but to withdraw from all of Asia Minor northwest of the Taurus Mountains.

Philhellenism

The Romans, whom the Greeks bitterly criticized as barbarians, were at least partly aware of their state's cultural deficiencies. While some Romans (Cato the Elder among them) deplored the influence of Greece on Roman life and culture with the opinion that it made the Romans morally weak and ethically decadent, others among the aristocracy embraced things Greek with enthusiasm. Those who did so were called 'Philhellenes'. An early example of the breed was Postumius Megellus in 282 BC, at the time when the Romans were expanding into southern Italy. Postumius addressed the people of Tarentum in Greek (though all he got for this courtesy were catcalls and abuse for his poor grammar).

Philhellenism received a major boost in 211 BC, when Marcellus took Syracuse. This resulted in the death of Archimedes, but also in the import of Greek statures, bronzes and paintings to Rome in the form of booty. The evident superiority of the Greek artefacts to their Roman equivalents caused a surge of interest in Greece and its intellectual and artistic achievements.

Consequently, when Fabius Pictor – who is generally considered Rome's first historian – wrote his *History*, the text was at least partly intended to explain Rome to the Greeks, and was also written in Greek. It helped that the Romans had no tradition of writing history, so Pictor turned to the Greek model. Being fluent in Greek (he had earlier been part of a Roman embassy to Delphi), it was natural that Fabius should write in that language. Before long, familiarity with Greek became essential for membership of the Roman intelligentsia.

Scipio Africanus, the conqueror of Hannibal, numbered himself among these Philhellenes, and while he was in Sicily this Roman general was often found relaxing in the Greek gymnasia and wearing a Greek cloak and sandals. Even the curmudgeonly Cato the Elder eventually came round and started learning Greek at the age of eighty. By then it was common for Roman aristocrats to trust their health to Greek doctors and their children's education to a Greek pedagogue.

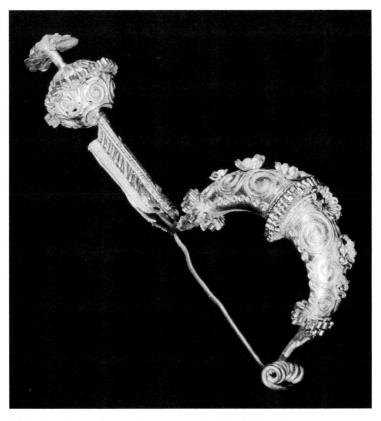

Fibula from Magna Graecia showing mixed Greek and Italian elements, *c.* 600–200 BC. These pins were used to hold together the shoulders of women's dresses.

The remains of the temple of Apollo at Syracuse, started 600 BC.

Roman tradition quickly absorbed the Homeric corpus, and it was around this time that the Romans began to develop the belief that they were descended from the Trojans whom Homer described in his *Iliad*. It also did not take long for the Romans to realize that many of their gods had the same attributes as Greek gods, not least because both sets of gods embodied the same natural forces. Through a process known as syncretism the two religions combined, until there was little difference between (for example) Minerva and Athena, or Diana and Artemis, other than their names. (However, cult practices still showed considerable variation.)

Where the Romans did not have the equivalent of a particular Greek god in their own pantheon, they simply adopted one. As early as 293 BC they realized that they needed a god of medicine and decided to adopt the Greek god Aesculapius in a formal ceremony. A temple was built for the god on Tiber Island, and it stood in Rome for the remainder of the Classical era. The Romans also adopted that very Greek god of art, culture and prophecy, which is why Apollo has no Roman name.

The Roman public were introduced to Greek culture through the plays of Aristophanes and Menander, although these were bowdlerized versions rewritten for a Roman audience by playwrights such as Plautus. (Given his wholesale plagiarism of Greek works, Plautus would hardly be entitled to complain that two of his plays were turned into classics of English literature by that equally profligate plagiarist William Shakespeare. Shakespeare's *Comedy of Errors* has the plot and some dialogue from Plautus' *The Brothers Menaechmus* and *Amphitryon*, and Falstaff is recognizable as Plautus' Miles Gloriosus from the play of that name – while Shakespeare's *Antony and Cleopatra* is largely drawn from the work of another Greek, the biographer Plutarch.) The Roman elite meanwhile ignored the Roman derivatives and preferred the Greek originals, which they watched in small theatres dedicated to Apollo. These were called Odeons.

Greek philosophy rapidly found fertile soil among Roman audiences, though the Romans were so outraged by the Sophists that they ejected them outright from the city. While Sophism concentrated on teaching excellence through rhetoric, the Romans saw only that Sophistic arguments could be used to make a fallacious argument prevail over the truth. (Even today a 'sophism' is regarded as a false argument designed to deceive the listener.) Stoicism, on the other hand, was exactly the sort of thing that the Romans could accept, and within two generations there were as many Roman Stoics as there were Greek.

The Romans already practised their own limited form of democracy, and the unrestricted Athenian version found little favour with a senate that already distrusted the 'demagogues' among their own people. It should also be noted that the 'pure' Athenian form of democracy was only ever practised in a minority of Greek cities, even at the height of the Greek democracy in the fifth century. Most Greek cities were oligarchies, or governments in which the popular vote was otherwise restricted. By the time of Roman rule no prominent intellectuals were making the case for Athenian-style democracy, which was generally regarded as a failed social experiment.

The end of the Hellenistic kingdoms

While the coming of Rome destroyed the Hellenistic kingdoms as political entities, the urban culture that had developed in the Middle East was to prove more durable. As so often, the Greeks opted for adaptation rather than absorption.

MACEDON

The fascination of the Romans for Greek art and culture did not develop into sympathy for contemporary Greeks. Rather, the Romans professed to admire the lost Greece of the time of Pericles, and regarded the Greeks of their day as 'Graeculi', quite literally 'lesser Greeks'. This was quite an assumption for the Romans to make of a people who were by some distance their betters in sophistication, wealth and territorial extent. However, the Romans were undoubtedly vastly superior in war, and having seen the benefits in wealth and prestige that came from waging war against the Greeks, the Romans wanted to do it more often. Command of wars against Hellenic states became a privilege eagerly sought by the Roman aristocracy.

Nor did the Greek kingdoms help their own cause. In money and manpower the Ptolemies and the Seleucids each had the Romans outclassed on their own, and the Macedonians (as the Romans reluctantly acknowledged) were almost as good at warfare. Had the Hellenic states seen the Romans as an existential threat and combined their forces, it is highly unlikely that the Romans could have withstood their joint onslaught. However, the Hellenistic kings had been preoccupied for centuries by their own internecine jousting for power and territory, and until it was too late they considered the Romans only as at worst distractions, and at best as potential assets in their constant warfare with their fellow kings. The Romans' conquest of Philip v caused as much rejoicing in the Ptolemaic court as did the later discomfiture of Antiochus iii. None of the

Hellenistic kings seems to have realized that these defeats were joint defeats by a power that would eventually overwhelm them all.

Perhaps the first to make this discovery was Perseus, the son of Philip v. Philip died with his kingdom diminished but still intact. Perseus was to see it implacably attacked and destroyed by the Romans. It did not help his cause that the Romans had favoured his brother Demetrios as successor to Philip, and Perseus had connived to gain the throne by forgery, lies and deceit. Convinced by Perseus that Demetrios was plotting against him, Philip had his innocent son executed, and even after discovering the truth Philip had no other heir to take Perseus' place. Perseus tried hard to mend the diplomatic bridges he had burned with the Romans, but to no avail. It suited the Romans to believe that he was plotting to restore the ascendancy of Macedon, and they dismissed his increasingly desperate attempts to make peace.

As ever, the war consisted of the Romans (opportunistically aided by the Pergamenes) attempting to get into Macedonia through the passes in Thessaly. Eventually the general Marcius Philippus did manage to blunder through by taking a route that no sane general would contemplate. His journey ended with his army trapped in a dead-end valley with no way back or forwards. Had Philip v been in charge of Macedon's army, the war might have ended right then with a massacre of the hapless Roman army. Instead, the less militarily competent Perseus panicked at the news that the Romans had entered Macedonia and pulled his troops back, thus leaving the Romans with a secure bridgehead into his kingdom.

The next year the Romans (under the command of the Philhellene Aemilius Paulus) advanced toward the Macedonian heartlands. Perseus met the Romans at Pydna, and that battle in June 168 BC proved once and for all that the flexibility of Roman military units made them superior to the powerful but unwieldy Macedonian phalanx. After this defeat Macedonian resistance collapsed, and the Romans made Macedon a client state; actually four client states, for the kingdom was broken into separate divisions to enfeeble it further.

The neighbouring state of Epirus now learned just how long the Romans held their grudges. More than a century earlier, Roman

Italy had been invaded by the Epirot king Pyrrhus. Now, using the excuse that Epirus had favoured Macedon in the recent war, the Romans turned on Epirus in a 'war' that was basically a huge plundering expedition. Over 150,000 Epirots were enslaved, and the country was so devastated that it never fully recovered.

The Macedonian war had one further consequence – the Romans no longer trusted the Greeks whom they had so recently 'freed', and as they withdrew their armies from the Greek mainland they demanded hostages from those states they trusted least. Among them was a young man called Polybius, who was to become the leading historian of his era. Polybius wrote with the intention of explaining to his fellow Greeks how Rome had so abruptly come to dominate the Hellenistic world. Naturally this text – one of the major surviving contemporary works of Roman history – was written in Greek.

SELEUCIA

Antiochus III died in 187 BC. Despite his defeat at Magnesia two years previously and the loss of Asia Minor, he still ruled a powerful kingdom that occupied the Levant and most of the Middle East. His son Seleucus IV spent much of his reign trying to contain the restiveness of his diverse subjects under the perceived military weakness of his government. This restiveness was not helped by the fact that Rome had demanded a massive indemnity as part of the peace terms, and taxes went up throughout the empire to pay for this. Seleucus even demanded money from the Jewish Temple of Jerusalem, thus rousing fierce anti-Seleucid sentiment among a people whom Antiochus III had kept resigned to his rule. This situation became even worse when Seleucus was assassinated and his younger brother Antiochus IV took the throne.

In 170 BC, just as the Romans were preparing their final blow against Macedon, Antiochus IV decided that the time was ripe for Seleucia to have another war with Egypt. His reasons were that Egypt was militarily weak and again ruled by a boy pharaoh (Ptolemy VI) who was controlled by feuding and incompetent 'advisors'. It was these advisors who provoked the war by an aggressive foreign policy perhaps intended to boost solidarity at home. Antiochus took the warlike posturing of the Egyptians at face value. He promptly invaded Egypt and set about dismembering its army. In the end he had most of Egypt under his control, though Alexandria held out against him.

Realizing the futility of continuing this war while he had restless eastern provinces in his own realm, Antiochus adopted young Ptolemy as his ward and left Egypt. This adoption was fair enough, since dynastic marriage arrangements had made the boy Antiochus' nephew, but the independent-minded people of Alexandria would not stand for it. They immediately promoted yet another Ptolemy (VIII) to ruler, forcing Antiochus back to the offensive.

Antiochus began by wresting Cyprus from Egyptian control, and then marched on Alexandria. He was met, not by a defending army, but by a lone Roman delegate. The Alexandrians had appealed to Rome, which had sent the young Popilius Laenas to turn back the Seleucid king. The Roman did not mince his words. Antiochus was told to either withdraw his army and return Cyprus to Egypt, or face war with the Romans. The king asked for time to consider his options, whereupon Popilius walked slowly around the king, drawing a line in the sand with his staff as he did so. Antiochus could take all the time he liked, the Roman said, but he must decide before stepping out of the circle. This insulting ultimatum was also a blatant show of strength that Antiochus had to respect. He withdrew and the sixth and final Syrian War (170–168 BC) came to an end.

Not unexpectedly, royal pride was severely bruised by this encounter with Rome. Therefore, when a Jewish mob, believing that Antiochus had died in Egypt, rioted and seized control of Jerusalem, the Seleucid monarch overreacted violently. Jerusalem was taken as though it was an enemy city. According to the Book of Maccabees (2 Maccabees 5) over 40,000 people were killed and an equal number enslaved.

While Maccabees represents the clash with Antiochus as a war of Jewish nationalism against a foreign oppressor, a closer look reveals that the conflict was as much a war between Hellenism and Judaism with large numbers of Jews on both sides. Not unexpectedly, Antiochus took the Hellenistic side and outlawed many Jewish religious practices while simultaneously and vigorously promoting the worship of the Olympic pantheon. Although outnumbered, the Judaic rebels were passionate about their cause, and a very nasty internal war developed.

To make things worse, the Parthians staged an opportunistic invasion that badly disrupted trade. Antiochus was forced to leave the Judaean mess to subordinates while he hurried east to meet this new threat. He had considerable success against the Parthians before succumbing to an illness that the Jewish rebels joyfully claimed as the smiting of the foe by their Lord.

This left the boy-king Antiochus v in charge, as his relative Demetrios (who had a better claim to the throne) was a hostage in Rome. Under Antiochus the empire struggled with a number of rebellions, but successfully subdued the Maccabean rebels and killed their leader. However, the Romans were alarmed by the size of the Seleucid fleet, which had been assembled partly for the Jewish war, and sent an ambassador to demand the fleet's disbandment. This the Roman did in typically blunt terms. The people of Antioch were still smarting from the treatment of Antiochus iv by Popilius. Now they demonstrated their disapproval of Roman tactlessness by rioting and lynching the ambassador. By way of retaliation, the Romans released the hostage Demetrios, who promptly returned to Syria and claimed his throne in 161 BC, disposing of young Antiochus in the process.

Demetrios awarded himself the title 'Soter', which meant 'Saviour', and by now his kingdom was in need of saving. The court was wracked by intrigue and dynastic infighting. Different factions struggled for support while rebellion broke out in Babylon. Meanwhile the Maccabees proved that they might be down, but they were not out, and they returned to the fight with new intensity while Demetrios was bogged down in a war in Cappadocia in Asia Minor. In 150 BC Demetrios was killed by a usurper supported by Rome (which by now had decided that Demetrios was an unsuitable protégé).

At this point the history of the Seleucid kingdom dissolves into a complex mass of civil wars, assassinations and coups, while the

Pompey, the future rival of Caesar, was also the man who finally brought to an end the Seleucid empire and stormed the temple in Jerusalem.

area controlled by its short-lived kings continually contracted as the different peoples of the diverse empire saw a chance to strike for independence. In the east such independence was short-lived, for the Parthians took every opportunity to snap up undefended or vulnerable territory, and the Seleucid kings were too weak and distracted to prevent this. When in 139 BC the Seleucids did attempt an attack on the Parthians, they were defeated, and the current king, Demetrios II, was captured. Meanwhile, through sheer persistence the Maccabean rebels had managed to secure a precarious independence for Judaea, as the Seleucid kings grappled with other priorities.

With the empire crumbling about him, Antiochus VII stepped up. Through a combination of diplomacy and intimidation he brought independent-minded provinces to heel, and controlled his court through sheer force of personality. He came to terms with the Jewish rebels, to the extent that they even contributed troops to his army as it marched east against the Parthians. Until 129 BC Antiochus VII led his army from one spectacular success to another. What this last great Seleucid king might have made of his empire will never be known. The Parthians killed him in an ambush, and with his death all the gains Seleucia had made in the past decade evaporated. The Parthians regained their lost territory, the Jews rebelled once more and, in an ominous new development, the kingdom of Armenia became both independent and expansionist.

By 100 BC the Seleucid 'empire' consisted of Antioch and a few nearby cities. Though largely irrelevant in even regional politics, the state continued to suffer from factional and dynastic struggles. Eventually, having crushed the Pontic king Mithridates VI, the Roman general Pompey took his army south and settled the turbulent Levant. In the process he almost incidentally abolished the Seleucid dynasty and made Syria a Roman province. Thus the empire founded in 334 BC came to an ignominious end 271 years later in 63 BC. Few mourned its passing.

HELLENISTIC ASIA

The collapse of Seleucia did not equate to the collapse of Hellenism in the east. In Anatolia the Greeks were dominant among the many ethnic groups that made up the culture of the region. The western kingdoms of Bithynia and Pergamon were almost entirely Greek

The stoa of Attalos, built in Athens in 159 BC and restored in the 20th century.

in culture and outlook, and indeed, the library at Pergamum (the capital of Pergamon) was generally considered second only to that in Alexandria. It was at Pergamum that a technique for preparing thin sheets of writing material from animal skin became popularized – allegedly because out of jealousy the Alexandrians were reluctant to allow the Pergamene library access to papyrus. Known to the Romans as *pergamenum*, and to the French as *parghemin*, this material is known today as parchment.

East of Pergamon the Greek cities continued to function as semi-autonomous entities within a dozen minor kingdoms. The value of Greeks in trade and manufacturing, and the capability of Greek mercenaries in the constant wars among these various kings, meant that the Greek population of each new kingdom was considered a prized asset. Kings made sure that the Greek cities received special treatment and tax breaks.

It was partly for this reason that the Greek cities of Asia led the – sometimes bitter – resistance to the spread of the Roman empire through the Middle East between 133 and 63 BC. While the kings of the region rightly saw the Greek cities as economic assets, the Romans treated them as urban piggy banks, to be squeezed dry by taxes. These taxes were already exorbitant before they were raised further by corrupt tax collectors working in collaboration with complaisant Roman governors. This created a cycle by which high taxes led to rebellions, which were put down to the accompaniment of punitive fines and even higher taxes, which led to further rebellions. After almost a century of this chronic misgovernment many of the cities of the east were economically devastated, and much of the population had left for the west, either to seek a better life or enslaved for the non-payment of debt.

Perhaps surprisingly, Hellenistic culture did best under the rule of the Parthian kings east of the Euphrates. These kings had nothing against Hellenistic culture and embraced many of its forms. Indeed, when the Roman general Crassus died in his failed attempt to conquer Parthia in 49 BC, the defeated general's head was presented to the Parthian king while he was watching a play written by the Athenian tragedian Euripides. Coins from contemporary Greek cities show on the obverse Greek themes in Greek writing, sometimes oddly at variance with the Asiatic king depicted on the face.

These Greek cities east of the Euphrates were to remain banks of knowledge that preserved the works of Greek thinkers and scientists even as the Roman empire crumbled to barbarism centuries later. It was in part the work of the early Greeks preserved in the East that sparked the age of Islamic science, and the rediscovery of these texts during the Crusades that launched the Renaissance in Europe.

Ptolemaic Egypt

The fall of the Seleucid empire left only one Hellenistic kingdom intact – Egypt. The survival of the Ptolemaic kingdom was based on two factors. The first was Egypt's geographical location, which made it very difficult to invade. The other was the foreign policy of the Ptolemaic kings, which was (to use a very broad generalization) based on giving the Romans whatever they asked for so as to deny them any excuse for coming to take it.

It helped that, despite the degenerate dynastic struggles that plagued all the failing Hellenistic kingdoms, the solid foundations laid down by the early Ptolemies kept the kingdom on an even keel. The Ptolemies worked hard to present themselves to the Egyptian people as native sons – and succeeded to the point that few people today realize that Cleopatra, the last Ptolemaic ruler of Egypt, was in fact a pure-bred Greek. By not only being sensitive to their people's religious sensibilities but enhancing religious worship with the addition of some splendid temple buildings, the Ptolemies made themselves generally accepted. A number of nationalistic rebellions showed that the Egyptian people were not totally convinced, but these rebellions were more against the misgovernment and incompetence of the later Ptolemies than against their non-Egyptian origins.

Three tactics were especially useful in keeping rebellions to a minimum. Firstly, the Ptolemies co-opted the priestly caste, leaving the rule of much of the state in their hands in return for an orderly populace and the prompt payment of taxes. Second, though the top jobs in the government were reserved for Greeks, the government was refreshingly non-racist in its definition of what made a Greek. Basically if someone spoke like a Greek, worshipped the gods of the Greeks and displayed sufficient familiarity with Greek culture, he was counted as a Greek even if his ancestors had never left the banks of the Nile.

Finally, the Ptolemies used a proto-feudal system for maintaining a Hellenistic core to their army by which settlers were given grants of land in exchange for military service. This core of dedicated soldiery was supplemented by levies from the Levant during those years that Egypt had a presence there, and the wealth of Egypt made it relatively straightforward to hire large numbers of mercenaries when the need arose. (This need arose essentially when there was conflict with the Seleucids; at other times the state was able to dispense with the expense of a standing army.) Native Egyptian troops were used to a much lesser extent, both because they were looked down on by the Macedonians and because they showed a distressing tendency to rebel once they had been trained.

These rebellions reached a peak under the weak rule of Ptolemy IV, when some districts broke away from the kingdom altogether

The Nile in a Roman mosaic, *c.* 2nd century AD. Egypt was considered a mysterious land, teeming with exotic wildlife.

Section of the Rosetta Stone. The inscription was written in the three languages shown here: Demotic, Classical Greek and Hieroglyphic, and this proved to be the key to the first translations of the last language.

and appointed their own 'pharaohs'. However, Ptolemy V brought the rebellions under control, though his was a strictly military solution that did little to address the underlying problems of resentment of high taxes and incompetent rule. Indeed, he proved both violent and treacherous, and did little to endear himself to his subjects. It was under Ptolemy V that a decree was published in three languages – Demotic (the standard written language of contemporary Egyptians), Greek and Hieroglyphic. A surviving chunk of this decree was discovered in Napoleonic times, and can still be seen in the British Museum. Known as the Rosetta Stone after the town where it was discovered, this decree proved the key for understanding previously untranslatable hieroglyphs. This opened several thousand years of Egyptian history to modern scholarship, making the Rosetta Stone one of the most significant finds in archaeological history.

Greece in Egypt

Alexandria was the Hellenistic capital throughout the period, but an older Greek city – the trading port of Naucratis – remained in business. If archaeology is any guide, Naucratis represented a better fusion of Greek and Egyptian cultures than Alexandria, as the city possessed some splendid temples to the Egyptian gods as well as to those of the Greeks. (Alexandria was segregated into Greek, Egyptian and Jewish quarters. None of these groups was very fond of the others, and riots and cultural strife were a constant feature of Alexandrian life throughout antiquity.) Much further up the Nile, Hellenistic Greece was represented by the city of Ptolemais, some 640 kilometres inland. Always an outpost of Hellenism, the city was intended by its founder, Ptolemy I, to serve as the regional capital of upper Egypt. Archaeology shows that the city had a Greek theatre, and temples dedicated to an eclectic mix of Greek and Egyptian gods.

These major settlements were surrounded by smaller towns with their own gymnasia and theatres. It may seem odd that such islands of Greek culture existed in a largely unchanged Egyptian hinterland, but the culture of the Greek city had evolved to allow isolated Greek colonies to flourish from the Crimea to Iberia, and Egypt was no exception.

The later Ptolemies indulged in warfare with a declining Seleucid empire and intensive diplomacy with Rome. Meanwhile the dynasty became locked in a series of internecine struggles in which rival claimants for the kingdom fought it out both in naval battles in the Mediterranean (Cyprus changed hands several times) and in diplomatic embassies seeking Roman support. The family infighting spilled over into a purge of intellectuals when Ptolemy VIII accused the Alexandrian intelligentsia of supporting a rival. He massacred and exiled dozens of academics, forever destroying the city's reputation for free-thinking research.

An interesting feature of later Ptolemaic rule is how often women (usually called Cleopatra) took power and ruled together with their husbands and sons. A good example is Cleopatra III, who married Ptolemy VIII (who was originally married to her mother, Cleopatra II). When Ptolemy died in 116 BC, Cleopatra ruled with her mother as regents for Ptolemy IX. However, Cleopatra minor decided that another son, Ptolemy X, was a better choice and she installed him as pharaoh instead. This proved an error, as after a few years Ptolemy X had his mother murdered and became sole ruler.

The Ptolemaic strategy of keeping on the good side of the Romans maintained the kingdom's independence until the middle of the first century BC. The problem then became more complex. By now – several rebellions and assassinations later – Egypt was ruled by the drunken Ptolemy XII ('the flute-player') and his daughter-regent Cleopatra VII (generally known to history as *the* Cleopatra). After her father's death Cleopatra was deposed following a series of palace plots involving her brother-husband Ptolemy XIII and ambitious and scheming courtiers.

Rome meanwhile was in the throes of a civil war between Caesar and Pompey. When the defeated Pompey fled to Egypt, Cleopatra was a semi-exile. Ptolemy XIII was in power, and he decided that the best way to ingratiate himself with Caesar was to kill Pompey and present Caesar with his rival's head. This was a severe miscalculation, and Caesar was infuriated rather than pleased by the murder. When Cleopatra had herself smuggled into his presence (allegedly rolled in a carpet), Caesar was easily persuaded to support her claim to the throne. So closely did the pair work together that they produced a son, usually referred to by historians as 'Caesarion'.

With Caesar's help, Cleopatra was restored to power after a brief but nasty war, but the period of stability that followed was transitory. Caesar was assassinated in 44 BC, and Rome was again thrown into turmoil. Cleopatra had little say in how matters turned out for Egypt, which was assigned by Roman politicking to be the ally of the triumvir Mark Antony. Again Cleopatra set to work closely with her new ally, and again so convivial did Antony find this collaboration that several children were born as a result of it.

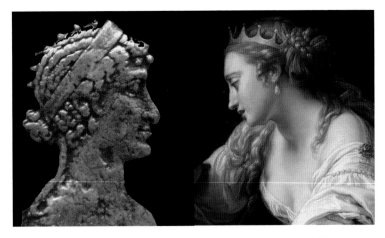

The two Cleopatras. A contemporary coin shows that Cleopatra wanted her subjects to see her as a mature, responsible ruler, rather than the femme fatale in this 18th-century painting by Pompeo Girolamo Batoni.

However, Cleopatra had allowed herself to become too closely identified with Mark Antony's faction. Antony's rival was Octavian, the man who was to become Rome's first emperor as Augustus Caesar. Claiming that Cleopatra had corrupted Antony and was seeking to rule in Rome with Antony as her puppet, Octavian declared war on Egypt, thus forcing Antony to come to Cleopatra's defence.

So it happened that the final war fought by Ptolemaic Egypt was a side effect of the struggle between two powerful Romans. When Mark Antony's cause went down in defeat along with much of his fleet at the Battle of Actium in 31 BC, the last independent Hellenistic kingdom went down with it. Cleopatra committed suicide to avoid being taken to Rome as a prisoner, and Egypt became a Roman possession.

After almost three centuries, the Hellenistic era was over.

SEVEN

GREECE IN ROME

'Captive Greece took her crude conqueror captive, and brought her arts to rustic Latium'. Thus declared the poet Horace in the last years of the first century BC (*Epistulae*, 2.1.156–7). By then 'Greece' meant the Roman provinces of Achaea and Macedon, and the population had suffered terribly in the civil wars fought by the Roman dynasts.

The armies of Sulla had fought the Pontic king Mithridates in Greece, and in the process Sulla had looted Delphi and sacked Athens. Caesar had defeated Pompey in Greece, and the assassins of Caesar had been brought to battle in Greece. Even Horace had fought in Greece, though he was a poor soldier. (He frankly admitted to having dropped his shield and run for his life.) The climactic battle of the civil wars, the Battle of Actium in 31 BC, which brought Augustus to power, was also fought just off the Greek coast. The result of the chaos and devastation wrought by these warring armies was described by a colleague of Cicero in a letter:

> On my voyage from Asia, as I was sailing from Aegina towards Megara, I began to look about at the places around me. Behind me was Aegina, in front Megara, on my right the Piraeus, on my left Corinth. All these were once thriving settlements, but now they lay before my eyes in ruin and decay.
> (Servius Sulpicius to Cicero, *Epistulae ad familiares*, 28)

While Asia Minor and other Greek possessions in the East did not suffer as badly as Greece from the fighting, the cities were wrecked financially by the insatiable demands of the Roman authorities for taxes and resources. Tens of thousands of people were unable to pay the exorbitant interest on their debts and were shipped to Rome as slaves, often alongside their confiscated assets. It took Asia Minor almost a century to regain the ground lost to the economic devastation of Rome's civil wars, and Greece itself never really recovered, remaining a provincial backwater for the rest of antiquity.

Yet, despite this, transplanted on to Roman soil, Greek culture thrived. A cultured Roman aristocrat of the Late Republic and Early Imperial period would have been practically bilingual in Greek and Latin and could (and often did) quote Homer at the drop of a hat. 'Ah, never to have married, childless to have died,' sighed Augustus, quoting the *Iliad*, when disappointed in his daughter, and coarsely remarking (again from the *Iliad*) 'that man's spear casts a long shadow' – a reference to a well-endowed naked fellow bather.

Indeed, one of Augustus' relatives by marriage was a former friend of the late Cicero who had the nickname 'Atticus', a name derived from his long stay in and lifetime fondness for Attica in Greece. Another protégé of Augustus was a shy young poet called Virgil, who took up the task of describing the origins of the Roman people in a verse epic derived directly from the *Iliad*. This poem – the famous *Aeneid* – draws directly and deliberately on Greek myth to create the legend that Rome was founded by a descendant of Venus (Aphrodite) who survived the Greek sack of Troy. The *Aeneid* is very consciously a continuation of the Greek mythological tradition in Latin, and the fact that this was possible shows how close Graeco-Roman culture was to becoming a single entity.

It became standard for a wealthy Roman to have in his atrium Greek statues, or at least excellent Roman copies thereof. We see signs of cultural dissonance when the Roman discomfort with nudity clashed with the Greeks' admiration for the naked human form. The Greek opinion slowly prevailed, with first the gods appearing naked in Roman statuary, then characters from mythology, dead heroes and finally living persons. As a result, when Augustus' wife, Livia, came unexpectedly on a group of naked men, she waved away any embarrassment by saying they 'seemed no more to her than statues'.

Cultural fusion. This statuette of a Greek goddess (Nemesis) from *c.* AD 150 is modelled on a Roman empress and found in Egypt.

Nevertheless, Rome did win one round in this cultural battle. While Greek statues were heavily idealized, the Romans went for the warts-and-all style of portraiture. The result and compromise can be seen in some statues (for example those in the Metropolitan Museum of Art in New York) where the wrinkled and balding heads of prominent Romans sit atop the muscled torsos of athletic teenage Greek bodies, and the stately heads of Roman matriarchs rest on the perfectly sculpted shoulders of nubile Greek maidens.

Something of the same compromise is seen in architecture. The Romans were fond of using concrete, a durable and flexible but unlovely material. Therefore many Roman buildings, both public and private, were solid bricks-and-mortar plus concrete, yet faced with Greek-style marble, and apparently supported by actually unnecessary columns. These columns were in the Greek architectural orders of the restrained Doric (Spartan) style, the more relaxed Attic (Athenian) style or the flamboyant Corinthian. Occasionally Roman buildings such as the Theatre of Marcellus or the Flavian amphitheatre (the Colosseum) would mix and match their styles, with a different Greek architectural order on each storey. The Greek origins of Roman architecture (the word itself is from the Greek *arkhitekton*) are plainly shown in this example from the text of the Roman Vitruvius in his book *On Architecture*:

> To the forms of their columns are due the names of the three orders, Doric, Ionic, and Corinthian, of which the Doric was the first to arise, and arise in primitive times, at that. When Dorus, the son of Hellen and the nymph Pythia, was king of Greece and all the Peloponnese, he built a fane [a small temple or shrine], which chanced to be of this order, in the precinct of Juno at the very ancient city of Argos, and after that he built others of the same order in the other cities of Achaea. (6.1.3)

The Romans were excellent builders, and their use of the arch and the three-dimensional arch (the dome) was far superior to anything produced by the Greeks. Yet so comprehensively had the Romans taken Greek architectural standards on board that they continued to make their buildings appear as Greek as possible. For instance, most public buildings had columns and architraves at the front – a style still used by Western architects today for public edifices such as government offices, banks, libraries and law courts.

Yet for all their enthusiastic adoption of themes from Classical Greece, the Romans still affected to despise contemporary Greeks, just as Cato the Elder had done before. (Cato the Younger, on the other hand, adopted the Greek philosophy of Stoicism so comprehensively that he is sometimes called 'Cato the Stoic'.) Thus, when Augustus was in Egypt, he went to pay his respects to the still-preserved body of Alexander in Alexandria. When asked if he also wanted to see the mausoleum of the Ptolemies, the emperor sneered, 'I came to see a dead hero, not a collection of corpses.'

Nevertheless, the reality was that Greece was winning all the way down the line on the cultural front. This is also shown by the fact that while Greek medicine, theatre, dress, cookery and education were becoming commonplace in the Hellenized Roman West, the already Hellenized East adopted very little that was Latin apart from the deplorable Roman taste for watching gladiatorial combat. While the Latin language was occasionally used in administration, *Koine* remained the common tongue of the eastern Roman empire,

Though in the Roman Forum, this temple of Antoninus Pius (constructed *c.* AD 158) has a Classical Greek frontage in the Corinthian style. The superstructure is a later addition.

and apart from a few administrators no one in the east bothered to learn Latin, not least because the Romans with whom they interacted already spoke Greek very well.

The one area where Greek culture was totally subsumed was in warfare. The Roman legions had proved conclusively that Rome needed only to be superior in this one aspect to become master of Greece, and the Greek phalanx and pikemen disappeared from history. Roman officers, who had more flexibility in their dress, might like to affect the style of earlier Greek warriors, but the style of warfare practised so enthusiastically by the Hellenistic kings had now vanished from the Mediterranean world.

The 'Roman' philosophers

In many ways the first century AD brought the passing of the intellectual torch from Greece to Rome, though in some other ways this is misleading. The Stoic philosopher Epictetus taught and wrote mostly in Rome, but he was a Greek who wrote in Greek and he eventually retired to the Greek east, whence he had been brought as a slave when he was young. Stoicism, with its emphasis on the individual and the irrelevance of externalities, appealed to aristocratic Romans, especially because their state was now under imperial management and they had much less say in events. Rome's senators quickly realized that the 'restored Republic' of Augustus was a sham, and that they actually lived under a disguised military dictatorship. However, Stoicism taught that no man was a slave unless he considered himself as such, and it was up to each person to decide how much he could bear.

This, one might assume, would make Stoicism appealing to the more oppressed classes in the empire, but as far as we know Stoicism was attractive mainly to the aristocratic class, and later even found a disciple of its teachings in the emperor Marcus Aurelius (AD 161–80). His *Meditations* (one of the few texts we have that was actually written by an emperor) contain numerous aphorisms, such as 'You have the power over your mind – not external events.' These could have been originally stated by Zeno in his stoa in Athens.

Another dedicated Stoic was Seneca, a courtier of Nero who was eventually put to death by that ungrateful tyrant. Seneca's *Letters to Lucilius* are essentially Stoic texts in which he freely admits the debt of his discipline to Greece. His *Letters* are larded with references to Greek philosophers and their theories, together with passages from Greek plays and Greek proverbs (all quoted, naturally, in the original Greek).

The politician and orator Cicero also fancied himself as a philosopher, and on those occasions when he was excluded from political life he consoled himself by writing philosophical texts. Mainly he was an Academic Skeptic, a student of the school of philosophy founded by Plato in Athens. As a Skeptic, Cicero was free to accept any argument he found convincing, and so could pick and choose from other philosophies that attracted him (mostly Stoicism). In the tradition of Socrates, Cicero was fond of using dialogues to establish an argument. He was less fond of Epicureanism, despite this being the philosophy of his philhellenic friend Atticus. It is partly Cicero's misrepresentation of Epicureans as dedicated to food, wine and sex that has given the modern Epicurean exactly that reputation.

Almost all Romans were familiar with the principles of philosophical discourse, not least because many young Roman aristocrats went east to study their philosophy at the source in Greece. Indeed, when the future emperor Tiberius decided that he had had enough of Rome (and of his licentious wife, Julia), he retired to the island of Rhodes, where

> He was a constant attendant at the schools and lecture-rooms of the professors of philosophy, and once when a hot dispute had arisen among rival sophists, a fellow had the audacity to ply him with abuse when he took part and appeared to favour one side. (Suetonius, *Tiberius*, 11.3)

Others, such as the Epicurean Lucretius, used the medium of poetry to expound some remarkably modern theories. Lucretius' six-part poem *De rerum natura* built on the works of the Greek philosopher Epicurus and covered matters as diverse as astronomy,

Francesco Zuccarelli, *Cicero Discovers the Tombstone of Archimedes*, 1747, oil on canvas.

atomic theory and evolution. As a source of scientific inspiration Lucretius was as important during the Enlightenment of the eighteenth century as he was in his own lifetime.

Thus it was with Greek philosophy as it was with Hellenism within the Roman empire. The Greek empire of the Hellenistic kings was gone, but Hellenism lived on as part of a greater whole, and Hellenism changed that whole much more than Hellenism was changed by it.

Two philhellenic emperors

We have already seen that many Romans of the Republic, such as Scipio Africanus, went out of their way to adopt aspects of Greek culture. This tendency continued when the Hellenic east had become part of the Roman empire. We have already seen that Tiberius was attracted to Greece. However, the first emperor to consciously strive to be as much a Hellenistic monarch as a Roman *princeps* is not the best example of the breed, for it was none other than the infamous

Nero. Certainly, after having seen the lamentable tendency of the later Hellenistic kings to be killed by those wives, children and other family members whom they had left un-executed, there is something familiar in Nero's murders of his wife, mother, stepbrother and (possibly) adoptive father.

With Nero, philhellenism was a reciprocal affair by which the emperor embraced Greek culture and in return bestowed the benefits of his rule mainly on the eastern parts of the empire. (There he was wildly popular, and his overthrow was mourned bitterly.) To his fellow Romans Nero justified his fondness for chariot-racing by pointing out that the heroes of the *Iliad* had also personally raced their chariots, and like Nero, these heroes were fond of performing on the lyre.

This latter penchant later came to be used against Nero in an almost certainly false rumour spread by his enemies; namely that while Rome burned in the great fire of AD 64, the emperor used the burning city as inspiration to compose an extempore poem on the fall of Troy. (The even more false report that Nero fiddled while Rome burned is easily discredited by the absence of fiddles in antiquity.)

Nero went further than most Romans in his fondness for Greek statuary and contemporary Alexandrian verse. However, he was pushing the limits in a direction in which the Romans were already going. Bilingual in Greek and Latin (he even addressed the Roman senate in Greek on occasion), the emperor was happier in places like Naples and with the culture of Magna Graecia than he was in Rome. Indeed, one of the reasons for his fall was that in the last years of his reign the emperor took himself on an extended tour of Greece, even though the deteriorating political situation urgently required his presence in the capital.

While he was in Greece, Nero bestowed 'freedom' on the peoples of that state itself. He made the significant remark that he would have preferred to do so while Hellas was in its prime, since now there were so few people around to enjoy it. This freedom consisted of tax breaks and a large degree of autonomy (which many cities promptly took as a licence for intercity rivalries and civil strife). It was promptly taken back when Nero's successor,

Vespasian, came to power and remarked that in his opinion 'The Greeks had forgotten how to be free.'

As the modern historian Miriam Griffin wrote in *Nero: The End of a Dynasty* (1987):

> In this period . . . 'Greek' was a linguistic and cultural classification embracing the inhabitants of Greek cities in Asia Minor, Syria, Palestine, Egypt and Cyrene. It was not only the Greeks of Achaea and Asia that looked to the ancient cultural tradition . . . The history of ancient Greece, too, was celebrated by writers from all over the Greek diaspora.

Thus Nero, in his fondness for things Greek, looked not only at the ancient roots in the Greek mainland, but at the wider world of ancient Greece. Indeed, when things got really bad, Nero considered fleeing Rome and making a career for himself as a lyre player in Alexandria.

Rome's most philhellenic emperor, Hadrian, was sometimes called *Graeculus* in ironic acknowledgement of the amount of attention he gave to the Greek east. This attention took the form of massive public benefactions including the restoration of roads, temples and baths, but it was also a determined attempt to make the Greek east a fully involved and participating part of the empire. Hadrian's sexual predilection for pubescent teenage boys was also seen by the Romans as typically Greek, though many of his Latin contemporaries shared his vice.

Educated in Greece, Hadrian was invited to become an Athenian citizen while he was emperor. He took up the offer and served as an Athenian Archon for a year. On his favourite city, Hadrian bestowed a number of temples and a library, as well as personally undertaking a reform of the city's laws. While Hadrian concentrated on making the Greeks partners in empire, he made no attempt to force western culture on the Greeks. Rather, he seems to have accepted that the empire had a western part and an eastern part, and these should each develop along their own lines. This was something of a departure for the Romans, who had previously seen the east as a resource to be exploited. It also marks the beginning of

Though very different in character, the emperors Nero (left) and Hadrian (right) shared a love of Greek art and culture, which they actively promoted throughout the empire.

the trend that eventually saw the Roman empire divided by the Greek language and culture on one side, and on the other a western portion that was a fusion of Greek, Latin and 'barbarian' cultures.

That Hadrian consciously refrained from cultural imperialism is shown most clearly by the one case in which he did not so refrain. This was in Judaea, where a sort of cultural civil war between Hellenized and conservative Jews had been simmering since the time of the Macabees. There had already been one outbreak of rebellion in AD 66, which (though the underlying causes were much deeper) was sparked by Greeks performing their sacrifices in front of a local synagogue, and Jewish sentiment was outraged by the philhellenic Nero's refusal to prevent the practice.

Likewise the rebellion under Hadrian had a number of economic and social causes, but the immediate impetus to armed revolt was when Hadrian visited Jerusalem in AD 130 and discovered that the city was still dilapidated from the Roman sack after the rebellion of AD 66–70. Jewish delight at Hadrian's proposal to rebuild the city soured rapidly when it was discovered that the emperor had a typical Hellenistic urban structure in mind, complete with baths, gymnasia and pagan temples. There is also a report of dubious veracity that Hadrian further planned to forbid the practice of circumcision, which, like most Hellenes, he saw as

This statue at Hadrian's palace in Tivoli reflected the idealized view of the Greek hoplite in the later Roman empire.

an act of genital mutilation (*Historia Augusta*, 'Hadrian', 14). This insensitivity resulted in a full-scale war lasting from AD 132 to 136 which saw the massacre and expulsion of tens of thousands of Jews. The vindictive Hadrian renamed Judaea, and probably deliberately chose to call it after the enemies of the Jews, that is, the Philistines, so the Roman name of the province was thereafter Syria Palestina. This created the Jewish-Palestinian division that has remained problematic ever since.

Heron of Alexandria

At about the time that the first Jewish War broke out, in AD 66, one of the last and most remarkable Greek scientists in Alexandria was just passing his prime. This was Heron, who like many of his scientific predecessors was an employee of the famous, and by now venerable, Library of Alexandria. While Heron never set his works into a formal text, the Library appears to have preserved many of his lecture notes. These were transcribed into Arabic after the fall of Greek Egypt, and only much later rediscovered by the West.

What makes Heron so interesting to modern readers is his interest in what appeared to be eclectic research in his day but is integral to twenty-first-century life. An example is his holy water dispenser in a temple. When a coin was inserted into a slot in this machine, it was guided on to a pan. If the coin was the right weight (the shape of the slot had already determined that it was the right size), the coin would tip a finely balanced scale to tilt the pan downwards. This would lift a gate on the opposite arm, allowing the holy water to flow into a container. Eventually the angle of the pan would be such that the coin slid off. The balance then returned to equilibrium, and the flow of water was cut off. In short, Heron had invented the coin-operated vending machine.

Heron also came up with an 'automobile', though one of limited practicality. This was a cart with a rope wound around the axle and attached to a weight. As the weight dropped, the rope unwound and moved the cart forwards. By winding the rope closer to the wheels on each side in sequence, Heron could make the machine move forwards and turn in a pre-programmed routine.

Heron might have taken this idea further had he integrated it with his aeolipile, which was the world's first steam engine. This was not developed by Heron, since there are earlier mentions of such devices, but he was the first to describe exactly how such a machine worked. The engine was basically a water-powered rocket that channelled the steam from boiling water into a ball with jets facing in opposite directions. As the steam exited under pressure, the ball revolved.

Heron's contemporaries regarded this machine as an interesting irrelevance, but they were more impressed by a device that opened temple doors by heating water so that the steam condensing in a container eventually developed enough impetus to pull the doors open. Similar adventures in hydrology created a fountain that operated by hydrostatic energy, and a force pump for water jets that was much appreciated by firemen.

In terms of pure mathematics, Heron also proposed a formula for discovering the area of a triangle. This was a significant advance in plane geometry. (First discover the semi-perimeter (s) by adding the length of the three sides and dividing this sum by two, then calculate the area as the square root of $s(s-a)(s-b)(s-c)$, where a, b and c are the sides.)

In other research Heron worked on levers and cranes, and how they might be developed into catapults as weapons of war. He also prepared a treatise on the nature of light (the *Catoptrica*), which discussed reflection and the discovery that light takes the shortest route between two points.

Christianity

Another first-century phenomenon that developed in the Greek east was to have huge implications later. This was Christianity. As a religious development Christianity was highly significant because it was (in contemporary eyes) a form of Judaism that was inclusive of Hellenism. Earlier forms of Judaism had required those embracing the belief to become Jews. Christianity, on the other hand, consciously aimed at being inclusive of the Greeks and other 'gentiles'. This demanded a certain degree of balance, for as St Paul commented, 'The Jews demand signs and Greeks seek wisdom', but the very fact that this comment comes in a letter to Christians in the Greek city of Corinth (Corinthians 1:20) shows that early Christianity was prepared to accommodate both camps.

In the Acts of the Apostles and in the travels of St Paul, we see how the infrastructure of the empire provided the means for propagating the beliefs of the new religion. These early preachers took advantage of the protection of Roman law (as in Paul's famous appeal to Caesar), and of the ability of the peoples of the Greek east to travel freely from city to city and to keep in touch by correspondence thereafter.

While Christianity rapidly gained a foothold in Rome, it spread most quickly through the Hellenistic world. This is why,

Tourist tat. A terracotta oil lamp showing the port of Alexandria. This lamp was probably sold to tourists and other visitors to the city in the imperial era.

although the original language of the Gospels is hotly debated, there can be no doubt that it was the Greek versions that received the widest propagation and which spread through the cities of the east. (Though originally there were a number of Gospels and these were whittled down to the definitive four only in the late second century – at the earliest.) As early as the first century AD we find Pliny the Younger, governor of the province of Pontus et Bithynia in Asia Minor, writing in some perplexity to the emperor Trajan, describing this new religion and asking his imperial master what he should do about it.

In later years, as Christianity spread through the empire and engaged the Roman upper classes, the question of how Christianity and Greek philosophical thought interacted led to a number of thoughtful discussions among the church fathers. Even today, there remains a lively debate as to how far Hellenistic thought has influenced Christian dogma. Stoicism, for example, holds many tenets so close to Christian thought that for many years it was believed that the Stoic philosopher Seneca was a closet Christian. It is however precisely because Christianity and Stoicism had so much in common that the former was able to gain a foothold among Rome's

This 3rd-century inscription from Rome mixes Christian icons and slogans (the Greek inscription reads 'the fish of life' with Roman paganism; the D. M. at the top stands for 'Dis Manibus' – 'to the spirits of the Underworld').

Hellenized elite – and this in turn led to the development of the Christian character of the late Roman empire.

The Roman empire: Greek east and Latin west

In the year AD 395 the emperor Theodosius I died. He was the last ruler of a united Roman empire, for he left his realm to two sons: Honorius, who was to rule the western portion, and Arcadius, who was put in charge of the east. This separation of the empire into two parts was only the formalization of a process that had been under way for many years, ever since the Greek east had come to be seen as part of the empire in its own right, rather than a means of channelling resources to the west.

It should be added that this change was by no means good for the western part of the empire, because the east had access to the trade routes to East Asia and had deeper roots in manufacturing and an urban economy. The west was poorer and more agricultural and, as a modern economist would put it, had a permanent balance of trade deficit.

The emperor Diocletian (AD 284–305) had been among the first to separate the empire into two parts, mainly because he needed commands in the east and west that could react immediately to the abundance of crises that threatened the empire of his day. Then the emperor Constantine built his 'New Rome' on the site of the former Greek city of Byzantium in AD 330. One of the main strategic purposes of siting the city on the Bosporus was to prevent the easy movement of hostile armies from west to east and vice versa. However, it turned out that in putting his city where he did, Constantine provided the future eastern empire with a ready-made capital. When the emperor Valentinian I decided to share the empire with his brother Valens, it was a natural choice for the more militarily competent Valentinian to take the struggling west, and to give Valens in Constantinople command of the east.

What is interesting about the Roman empire after its formal division on the death of Theodosius is how precisely the eastern portion followed the borders of the Hellenistic kingdoms that the Roman empire had replaced. The Diocese of Egypt was more or less the Ptolemaic kingdom – including Cyrenaica – and the dioceses of Thrace, Dacia and Macedonia combined to re-form what had once been the Macedonian kingdom of the Antigonids. The Diocese of the East combined with the dioceses of Pontus and Asia (Minor) to make up the old Seleucid kingdom (apart from those areas in the east originally lost in the Parthian rebellion).

In short, in the eastern Roman empire, the dream of Antigonus the One-eyed was realized – five hundred years later. Apart from the lost eastern kingdoms, the realm of Alexander the Great was again united under a single ruler. This empire called itself Roman, but was Greek in language and culture. Though the western Roman empire had less than a century to go before its final demise, the eastern one would endure for another thousand years.

EIGHT

Byzantium and the End of the Greek East

As with the word 'Hellenism', the term 'Byzantine' for the Greeks in the east was coined by later historians. The people of the Byzantine empire called themselves Romans, though they said and wrote the word in Greek.

For much of the late antique and medieval era, Byzantium was the strongest power in the Mediterranean region, both economically and militarily. As a result the empire acted as a buffer between the debilitated west and the new powers developing to the east. The Byzantine empire created little that was new in the scientific and philosophical fields, but the civilization served as a repository of the achievements of earlier eras, preserving much of the work of scientists and writers such as the histories of Thucydides and the works of Archimedes. Architecturally, the Byzantine legacy – best illustrated by the awe-inspiring Hagia Sophia, which remains the most impressive building in modern Istanbul – can be seen throughout the Middle East and central Europe, from Syrian mosques to Austrian churches.

As it happened, the legacy of Byzantium endured more in those parts of Europe that were never under the empire's control than it did in the eastern lands it ruled. Over time the Byzantine empire lost its Roman characteristics, and both reverted to its Hellenistic roots and absorbed much of the culture of the Islamic powers that replaced it in the Middle East and Egypt. The influence of Byzantium and western culture remained and evolved in the lands conquered by Islam. By the ninth century, as well as exchanging blows on the battlefield, Muslims and Byzantines were

This church in rural Austria shows the far-reaching effects of styles of Byzantine architecture, which also heavily influenced the Baroque style.

exchanging knowledge on topics such as medicine, mathematics, astronomy and geography.

Byzantine art is justifiably famed, and its influence spread far beyond the lands of the empire. The effects can be seen in areas as diverse as Russian iconography and Persian mosaics. The art of Byzantium itself was primarily religious, because for many years the empire was the major bulwark of the Christian faith. Even as the lands of the east were lost to Islamic invasion, the Greek church was spreading its faith among the Rus, the Bulgars and the other warrior tribes of the northeast. Today, at a very rough estimate, the Greek orthodox church has some 200 million adherents, mainly in Russia, eastern Europe and Greece. The Cyrillic alphabet – developed by the Christian followers of the Byzantine saint Cyril – is a mix of Greek and Slavonic characters that forms the basis of written languages in Eastern Europe, Eurasia and the Balkans.

Prologue: heirs to Rome

Several factors prevented the eastern Roman empire from collapsing as the west had done. The two most important were military and economic. In military terms, although the armies of the eastern empire were no better than those of the west, they had an easier job. It has been repeatedly mentioned how defensible Ptolemaic Egypt was, and this remained the case in later years. The main threat to Egypt had been the Seleucid empire, and even this threat was removed in the Byzantine era as the peoples of the former Seleucid empire were now on the same side as the Egyptians.

The Levant and Syria was one of the more vulnerable areas of the eastern empire, but even here, the only hostile access was from the east. The Mediterranean was to the west, friendly Anatolia was to the northwest and Egypt was to the south. Even from the east, access for an invader was through a series of desert oases. This meant that any attacker had to provision his armies with a long and vulnerable supply chain. Going the other way, this factor had prevented the Romans from holding territory in Mesopotamia, and now the same circumstances hindered invaders hoping to advance to the west.

Anatolia itself was surrounded on three sides by water, with the narrowest strait and most vulnerable crossing point comprehensively guarded by Constantinople in the west. To the south was the Mediterranean, to the north the Black Sea, and to the east formidable mountain ranges with easily defended passes.

Therefore, while the armies of the west had to defend the long, easily crossed river frontiers of the Rhine and Danube, the

Zeno the Isaurian (425–91), whose reign did much to stabilize the eastern empire, as seen on a contemporary coin.

armies of the east were much better protected by geography, and could therefore respond more effectively to such threats as could develop. Yet, thanks to the Mediterranean, the eastern empire had excellent interior lines of communication that allowed it to deploy troops speedily to meet invaders or quash civil unrest. Because the provinces were safer from devastation by barbarian invasion and civil war, they remained economically productive and thus better able to pay for the armies deployed for their defence.

Furthermore, once separated from the western empire, the east was more easily able to balance its books. With civilization deeper rooted in the east, in part thanks to the long-entrenched urban culture of the Greeks, manufacturing was more widespread, as was a mercantile culture interested in trading these goods for profit. Furthermore, while all the west had on its borders were barbarian wildernesses, the east had trade access to the wealthy civilizations of China and India (among which we can now include the lost Greek kingdom of Bactria). Throughout this period trade flowed along the Silk Road and across the Red Sea with the monsoon trade winds. The only culture the Byzantines did not trade with was their fellow Christians to the west, and this was because the impoverished west had almost nothing to offer.

In the early years after the fall of the west, three great cities dominated the east: Constantinople in the north, Antioch in Syria and Alexandria in the south – two Hellenistic foundations and a Roman foundation on a former Greek city. Of these cities Constantinople faced the greatest threats, and its walls were correspondingly massive. These walls were added to and embellished by various emperors, so that after a thousand years, an awed witness – one Manuel Chrysoloras, himself a military man –wrote:

> I am unable to say in what the circuit and enceinte [the wall enclosing a fortified place] of the walls of Constantinople may not be superior to those of Babylon. The multitude of towers which crowned them was innumerable, their grandeur and height were such that one of them only would have sufficed to astonish the sight of the spectator and any man would have admired the great stairways and the imposing massiveness

Flask and donkey-holder, both made of blue-green glass (now brown through weathering). Real-life donkeys with large burdens were a common sight in contemporary 6th-century Byzantium.

of their construction. The doors of the towers were not less beautiful; the same may be said of the counter-murs [a backup wall, in case the wall in front is breached], which in any other city would have sufficed for its defence.

Moreover, the width and depth of the ditches which surrounded them were such that the quantity of water contained in them made Constantinople like a city surrounded by water.

The difficulty of storming Constantinople was evident even in an earlier age. A would-be barbarian invader from the west, Fritigern the Visigoth, drew his horde up before the walls of Constantinople after he had defeated the Romans at Adrianople in AD 378. Unable to find a way past the city to the east, and unable to attack the city itself, he withdrew, muttering sulkily that he 'kept peace with stone walls' – a policy he had maintained ever since his army had been comprehensively drubbed elsewhere before a set of greatly inferior fortifications.

Thus the fall of the Latin west – traditionally dated to AD 476 – was matched to some degree by the resurgence of the Greek east. Indeed, under the emperor Justinian I (527–65), the empire made a determined attempt to regain its lost lands. Justinian first proved the point that the eastern empire was highly defensible by beating back the Sassanian Persians, an aggressive empire which had risen in the east after Parthia collapsed under repeated barbarian and Roman assaults. He then turned his attention to Italy and north Africa, both of which were successfully reconquered (though at huge economic and human cost).

The Byzantine project to restore the empire was halted by a series of catastrophic natural disasters. Firstly, there came a bout of debilitating climate change. The cause is not certain, though a major volcanic eruption in Central America is the most likely suspect. The dimmed sunlight and sulphuric atmosphere that affected summers for several years proved to be incapable of sustaining crops, and famine was widespread. A decade later, the empire was hit by one

Byzantine troops defend Constantinople (detail from the *Skylitzes Codex*, a 13th-century manuscript).

of the most devastating plagues in known history. This plague was probably bubonic, and it was the first time the Middle East and Europe had encountered this. Lacking any immunity, people died by the million, decimating the manpower of the army and the economy that supported it. Just as the empire was recovering from these shocks, Phoenicia was hit by a massive earthquake, which according to one contemporary commentator killed 30,000 in Beirut alone.

By 560 the eastern empire was struggling to keep itself together, and the impetus for western conquest was gone. This was reflected in a decree by one of Justinian's successors, an emperor called Heraclius. Under Heraclius all official correspondence in the empire was written in Greek, and Latin as a language became largely obsolete. The eastern Roman empire might still call itself by that name, but, as later historians have recognized, this empire was a different entity and as such is given a different name. This was the Byzantine empire. It was Christian and Greek, and consisted almost entirely of lands conquered by Alexander almost a millennium previously.

An empire ebbs away

The story of the Byzantine empire over nine hundred or so years is the story of the slow ebb of Greek control over the lands they had occupied for so long, and its replacement by the Muslim culture that is today dominant in most of the Middle East, Egypt and the Levant.

The reign of Heraclius mentioned above was significant for another reason. At this time the Romans and Sassanian Persians fought a long, debilitating war in which both the Levant and Egypt were briefly conquered by the Persians. At one time the Persians advanced as far as the gates of Constantinople, but like invaders before and since they were unable to make any impression on the city's mighty walls. Thereafter a major effort by the empire regained Byzantium its lost lands. The effort of the war left the Persians and Byzantines financially and militarily exhausted. It was at this point that a new and completely unexpected player arrived on the scene.

Illustration from the 19th century which gives a good depiction of the dress of upper-class Byzantine men and women in the period AD 300–700.

When Heraclius celebrated the hard-won Byzantine victory over Persia in 629, he was aware that the Arabian Peninsula had been united under the prophet of a new religion. However, that prophet, Muhammad, had died in 620, and no doubt the Byzantines hoped the new threat would quickly dissipate. Instead, under the formidable Abu Bakr, the Arab forces grew yet more formidable and expansionist. At first it seemed as though the Arab expansion would be aimed at the Sassanian empire, and both Jews and Greeks living in those lands initially welcomed invaders who appeared as liberators from an increasingly repressive Sassanian regime. (Weakened by their long war with the Byzantines, the Sassanian Persians eventually collapsed under the Arab assault.)

Within a few years it became clear to the Byzantine authorities that, with the crippling of the Sassanians, their empire had seen one enemy replaced by another just as formidable. Lands that had once been Greek and then Persian were now dominated by Arabs bearing the new faith of their prophet.

Then, in 633, the Arabs advanced on Syria. Though the Byzantine empire was weakened by the long war with the Sassanians, it remained the top military power of the day. The problem was that the Byzantine generals both underestimated the Arabs and were unable to realign their strategic thinking to recognize that this threat was coming from a completely new direction. Our sources for the period are confused and fragmentary, but it appears that the

Byzantines were reluctant to commit their full strength against the Arabs. They wanted to keep much of the army in the usual positions to repel a conventional invasion from the east, and also had to keep troops in the north following violent incursions by Avar and Slavic tribes.

Furthermore, the Byzantines failed to realize that the Arab familiarity with desert conditions would enable them to pull off a flanking march that allegedly involved a two-day journey without water across the Syrian desert. Caught off-balance, the Byzantines were unable to prevent the loss of Palmyra and Bostra. Then, on 30 July 634, Byzantine and Arab armies met for a pitched battle at Ajnadayn, a location that is now unknown but is somewhere near the centre of modern Israel. The result was a major victory for the Arab forces and the loss of a good part of the Byzantine army.

The Arabs now drove for Damascus, defeating Byzantine forces sent against them piecemeal to give the city time to prepare for siege. After a siege of six months Damascus also fell to the invading army. Abu Bakr died in the siege, and command passed to the Caliph Umar. Despite stubborn Byzantine resistance and numerous battles, the Levant fell under Arab control, followed soon afterwards by Palestine. In 636 the city of Emesa (present-day Homs) fell. With the fall of the city founded by Seleucus I and where two emperors of Rome's Severan dynasty had been raised, western Syria fell largely under Arab control.

A massive Byzantine push to regain control of Syria resulted in the climactic six-day Battle of Yarmouk in 636. This historic battle represented the turning point in the long history of Greek control of the region. The Byzantines were defeated, and with this Arab victory, Greek control of the Levant and Syria came to a permanent end. The Byzantines were driven back as far as Anatolia, where the terrain favoured a defensive war, and there they were able to hold their ground. Over the coming decades, both sides plotted further invasions to regain lost lands or take further territory, but the border of the Byzantine empire was now effectively the Taurus Mountains of southeastern Anatolia.

Egypt

To this point Egypt had been under foreign control for almost a millennium. Since 323 BC the country had been controlled by the Ptolemaic dynasty. With the death of Cleopatra VII in 30 BC the country began a long period of Roman rule, which shifted without fanfare to become Greek once again as Egypt came under the control of first the eastern Roman empire and then the Byzantines. These changes of government were hardly noticed by the people of the country, because their administrators had always used Greek and Demotic as the language of government, and most of the actual governing was subcontracted to the priestly caste. Also, despite the changing management, the laws and customs of the country remained the same. Consequently, Egypt remained a relatively peaceful land untroubled by the civil wars and barbarian invasions that changed the rest of the civilized world.

All this ended in 618 with the Sassanian invasion and conquest, and the subsequent reconquest by the Byzantines under Heraclius. This was followed by the Arab invasion and conquest of the Levant, which left Egypt cut off and vulnerable. It was not long before the expansionist Arabs moved against Egypt, which was now an isolated outpost of Byzantine power. In 639 a small Arab force crossed from Gaza, and found that instead of stubborn resistance, local towns offered grudging submission or even a cautious welcome. The governor of Egypt was well aware that reinforcements from Constantinople would be few and slow in coming, and he tried desperately to negotiate and delay the invaders. Where the locals did feel strongly about the Arab invaders they were often able to fight them off, owing to the small size of the force involved. Even when reinforcements of veteran troops from the Syrian Wars arrived, the total army of the Caliphate numbered fewer than 14,000 men.

With his territory crumbling away piecemeal, the Egyptian governor asked for terms. Subject to consent from Constantinople, he was prepared to acknowledge Muslim suzerainty over Egypt and allow the people either to convert to the new religion or pay a head tax in lieu. This compromise made the Coptic Christians (including the governor) neutrals in the struggle, or even collaborators with

Byzantine art is immediately recognizable by the staring, distant expressions of its subjects, as in this mosaic of Christ from the Hagia Sophia.

the invaders. When the emperor Heraclius, as expected, indignantly rejected the peace terms, the invaders made a push to Alexandria, which came under siege in 641.

Alexandria was the embodiment of the Greek presence in Egypt, and the Byzantines were prepared to fight hard to keep it. Also, the city itself was well fortified and defended. It could be reinforced and supplied from the sea, so, given the political will to hold the place, this city could have held out indefinitely. In fact, it lasted six months.

That is because the Byzantine emperor Heraclius died just as he was preparing forces to come to the city's relief. The momentum to relieve Alexandria was dissipated in the palace infighting that followed, and Heraclius' successor survived only a few months himself before dying of illness. Abandoned and demoralized, the Alexandrians were unable to resist a determined Arab assault that captured the city. Thereafter, like the Levant and Syria, Egypt was permanently lost to the empire. Of the Greek east that had once stretched as far as the foothills of the Himalayas, only Asia Minor remained. Even Greece itself had largely fallen to barbarian invaders, though Athens was stubbornly held – more for the city's historical significance as the cradle of Greek culture than for any strategic value.

The shrinking empire

Byzantium was under pressure from tribes to the north, including the newly aggressive Rus, and still fighting hard to hold off the aggressive Caliphate. In 674 the Arabs made a determined attempt to capture Constantinople itself. The city held out, largely because of its impressive walls and a final flowering of Greek science. This produced a substance called 'Greek fire', which came to be dreaded by Byzantium's enemies. Greek fire was a petroleum-based liquid that was pumped through hoses under pressure. When lit, it resisted all attempts to douse it, and indeed it even burned on water, which made it a fearsome weapon when used against wooden ships.

Inevitably, the pressure of constant war told upon the population of the empire. Frequent raids by barbarians or the armies of the Caliphate forced the abandonment of some towns, and the loss of subsidized Egyptian grain meant that the huge population of Constantinople now shrank dramatically. By the eighth century, north Africa had been lost, and the empire consisted of Asia Minor, Sicily and a few holdings on the coast of Greece and Italy.

However, the Byzantine empire possessed a surprising resilience. After each major defeat it somehow struggled back, and though with each recovery it had less territory than before, substantial amounts of lost ground were regained. Thus the ninth and tenth centuries brought a resurgence under the so-called Macedonian dynasty under which all of Greece was reclaimed by the empire. Later expansion saw this European empire grow even further until

'Greek fire' was a top-secret weapon that the Byzantines used with devastating effect on enemy fleets. The caption to this picture reads: 'The fleet of the Romans setting ablaze the fleet of the enemies.'

under Basil II (976–1025) all the lands south of the Danube – Greece, Dalmatia, Macedonia and Thrace – were again under Byzantine control, along with much of southern Italy.

As Europe grew more prosperous, the empire was able to re-establish trade with the now-reviving west, while increased military power allowed the provinces to be defended and kept safe from the economic disruption of warfare. While the population of Constantinople climbed back to its former levels and the nobility prospered in a state that was once again the richest and most powerful in the region, the peasantry remained in a condition close to serfdom. Religious debate had largely replaced scientific investigation and philosophy, and while souls may have been enriched by this change, intellectual growth languished. Furthermore, peace and security bred a degree of complacency, so the empire was again unprepared when yet another hammer-blow struck from the east.

The Seljuk Turks and the end of empire

In the ninth century the Seljuk Turks were a tribe on the fringes of the Muslim world. They occupied an area around the Caspian Sea, but later moved south and converted to Islam. From there they began a steady expansion that would have been familiar to the Achaemenid Persians, the Greeks under Alexander, and the

Seleucids and Parthians. Once again the empire of Alexander was reunited under new management, though by this time there was little that was Greek about it.

Once the Turks had established their rule over the Levant and Egypt, their next target was Asia Minor, which remained under Greek control. Consequently, in 1065 the Seljuk and Byzantine empires clashed over this, the last eastern Greek possession. In 1071 the Byzantines risked everything on a major battle near Manzikert in which their army of some 50,000 men faced an enemy roughly estimated as being half the size. However, much of the Byzantine army was composed of peasant levies and mercenaries, and furthermore, poor generalship and political disagreements prevented the army from being deployed effectively. While many of the levies and even some of the mercenaries fled the battlefield, the emperor and his famed Vangrian Guard of Nordic mercenaries were surrounded. Most of the guard were killed and the emperor was captured.

The captive emperor was Romanos IV. He was treated kindly by the Turks and released for a ransom. His fellow Byzantines were less hospitable, and on his return Romanos was deposed, blinded and expelled from Constantinople. Soon afterwards he died of his injuries. The loss of the battle of Manzikert meant that the Byzantines were unable to stop the migration of the Seljuks into Asia Minor. This migration forever changed the cultural make-up of the

Map of the Byzantine empire prior to the Seljuk invasion.

country, which then began its evolution into the Turkish state that exists today.

Also at this time, the Normans (the same people who were to conquer Britain in 1066) succeeded in pushing the Byzantines out of southern Italy. Therefore in the early twelfth century the Byzantine empire consisted mostly of Greece plus Constantinople, though the empire still held grimly to the western seaboard of Asia Minor. Nevertheless, the Greek world was now smaller than it had been for two thousand years – and it was about to get smaller. The killer blow came not from the east this time, but from the west.

It was to some degree ironic that Byzantium had, over the centuries, shielded western Europe from the Caliphate, the Rus and the Turks as well as a host of less serious prospective invaders. As Europe recovered from the debilitating effects of the collapse of the western empire, barbarian invasion and plague, its economy was stimulated by trade with Byzantium, which brought increased prosperity to the region. The merchants of Venice and Genoa were deeply involved with this trade.

One sign of the increased strength and self-confidence of the west was the Great Schism – the separation of the Greek Orthodox and Catholic churches. In 1054 Pope Leo IX demanded that the eastern church recognize his supremacy. His contentious legation to Constantinople ended with the protagonists on each side excommunicating one another. This was followed by a slow split of the church as incompatible doctrines and practices developed over centuries of separation – a separation that has endured despite repeated attempts at reconciliation.

Also in the eleventh century a reinvigorated Europe launched its first counter-attack on the Muslims with the first Crusade, which recaptured the Holy Land (the Levant and much of what is today Israel). The Byzantines used this impetus to regain some lost ground in Asia Minor, especially along the Black Sea coast.

In 1198 the Crusaders planned a further attack, this time to regain control of Egypt. However, Egypt remained a crucial link along the Silk Road, which formed the basis of Venetian prosperity. Venetian merchants worked expertly with the diverse and conflicting political interests of the leading Crusaders to pervert the attack on Muslim Egypt into an assault on Christian Constantinople. Despite the horrified protests of the Pope, Constantinople was captured by the crusaders and comprehensively pillaged.

This sack in 1204 was a blow from which the Byzantine empire never recovered. The Venetians attempted to hold the city, but their grip was feeble and Constantinople was retaken by the Byzantines after the Crusade had lost its momentum. Crippling taxes were levied on the peasantry to pay for repairs to the city and for a military force capable of defending the remnants of the empire, but the effort caused hardship, rebellion and civil war. The empire was already in a state of collapse when the Ottoman Turks launched an attack on the enfeebled remains of Constantinople in 1453. The massively outnumbered defenders of the city stood no chance, and the last Byzantine emperor, Constantine XI, died in hand-to-hand fighting on the walls.

A few remnants of the empire remained, but essentially the fall of Constantinople brought to an end the Greek presence in the east and the wider Mediterranean world – a presence that had endured for millennia. With the loss of Byzantium, the Greek world had gone, and gone so comprehensively that within a few centuries few remembered that it had even existed.

EPILOGUE:
THE GREEK LEGACY

W ho were the Greeks? It may seem strange that we can properly approach this question only after an entire book about the lost empire of the Greeks. Yet through the text we have seen 'Greekness' described in many different ways, and discovered that what it was to be 'Greek' depended less on the status of an individual and more on who was asking the question and why.

Even in the prehistory of Greece, the question of Greekness was debated. The original peoples of Greece considered the Dorians as interlopers and invaders, for all that the Dorians maintained that, as the descendants of Hercules, they had a right not only to be in Greece but to dominate a large part of it. The Dorian question is still open today, with some ethnologists arguing that the Dorians were always a part of the original population and others claiming that they were foreign invaders who were absorbed by the culture of the people whom they invaded. (The Nazis, who admired the Greeks and especially the Dorian Spartans, claimed not only that the Dorians were invaders, but that these invaders were Aryans from central Europe.)

Nor do the Dorians raise the only question of ethnicity that remains unresolved. The Greeks before Alexander were reluctant to grant the status of Hellenes to the ancient Macedonians, and a number of academics obdurately hold that position today. Other academics use similarities in language, culture and religion to claim that Macedonians and Greeks were largely the same people,

Drinking cup from 8th-century Greece, showing warriors and horses. The strange shape of the warriors is because they carried shields pinched in at the middle.

albeit with different traditions. The creation of a modern state called 'Macedonia' has helped to fan the flames, even though modern Macedonia is not a part of the original Macedonian kingdom, which is actually in Greece.

One thing is reasonably certain, and this book should have helped to make it more so. Being Greek did not ever entail actually being born or residing on the Greek mainland. A host of Greek writers, inventors and philosophers were born and lived most of their lives outside the Greek mainland without anyone – ancient or modern – questioning their Greekness. No one thinks of Herodotus, Sappho or Homer as being anything less than Greek, though tradition claims that the first two came allegedly from Greek islands, while Herodotus was definitely born in Asia Minor. Archimedes was born in Syracuse and Pythagoras lived most of his life in southern Italy while both remained very much Greeks.

In any case, for a while the subject of the Greekness of the Macedonians became moot, because Alexander and his heirs had conquered the rest of Greece. If the nation's new rulers held that the Macedonians were Greek, their southern subjects were in no position to disagree. Furthermore, the question of who was Greek had assumed a wider dimension. Within the Hellenistic kingdoms of Asia Minor and the Middle East there was a diverse population of native peoples, some very different from one another. 'Greeks' – be they from Macedon or points further south – intermarried with these native peoples; indeed, from the beginning Alexander actively encouraged this.

At what point did someone with non-Greek blood cease to be Greek? The Greeks very sensibly chose not to go for genetic hair-splitting of the type that has people in the present-day USA deciding who is 'white' or 'black'. The Greeks opted instead for what in today's parlance we might call 'self-identification'. That is, if a person spoke Greek, was intimate with Greek culture, practised Greek religion and called himself Greek, then that person was to all intents and purposes a Greek.

This represented a changed approach from the Classical era, when Greek cities were very reluctant to give citizenship to – and thus bestow 'Greekness' on – outsiders. By this argument one could no more become an Athenian than a dog could become a cat. However, this approach was impossibly parochial in that not only foreigners but Greeks of impeccable Greekness could not change citizenship from that of their native city. With the Hellenistic kings founding new cities wholesale across their new conquests (Alexander alone founded well over a dozen cities), this definition collapsed rapidly. It was informally replaced by the more open and flexible definition given above, to the point where – for example – the Maccabees of Judaea were at war with 'Hellenes' who were every bit as Semitic as themselves.

Under the Roman empire 'Greekness' took a new turn. Now, even though they spoke and wrote in Greek, and originally prac-tised religious rituals that would have been immediately recognizable to their Hellenic ancestors, even genetically pure-bred 'original' Greeks called themselves 'Roman'. They continued to do so even after Rome itself was part of an alien kingdom, Latin was an obsolete language and the state had very little in common with the original Roman empire. It was only with the end of the Byzantine empire that the Greeks once more became such, and by then they had politically vanished altogether.

The Greek legacy

After the fall of Constantinople, even the idea of 'Greece' went into a period of eclipse. Most of the Greek mainland became part of the Ottoman empire, a huge state that dominated not just Greece but lands to the north, Egypt and most of the southern Mediterranean coastline. The Ottoman hinterland was most of the former Seleucid empire in Syria, Iran and Babylonia. Those Ionian islands that were not part of the Ottoman empire were held, ever more tenuously, by the Venetian Republic.

Although subsumed within the Ottoman empire, the Greek people were not absorbed by it. While the landholding classes had become largely extinct, a thriving merchant and business class came to replace them. This survives today in the entrepreneurial spirit of modern Greeks. However, many Greek intellectuals chose to leave the Ottoman empire altogether and fled to the west, taking with them whatever works of art, literature and philosophy they could.

Within the Ottoman empire, Greek culture also left its mark, which is why examples of Byzantine-style architecture are found far to the east in places such as Baku in Azerbaijan, where the Byzantines themselves never reached. The 'Turkish bath' is in fact a form of the Roman baths, preserved by Byzantine culture and passed on to the Ottomans (who adjusted the *hammam* slightly to fit with the needs of their religion).

The Parthenon in Athens was an iconic combination of Greek architectural genius and artistic beauty. Therefore it is perhaps fitting to use its fate as a symbol of the fate of Greek independence during the Ottoman occupation. The original Greek temple had become a Catholic church and then, under Turkish domination, a mosque. During the seventeenth-century wars between the

Venetians and Turks the building was used as an arsenal, perhaps because the Ottoman garrison of Athens believed that the westerners would not fire on a building of such great worth. In this they were mistaken. Either by accident or by design a Venetian mortar shell was lobbed right into the middle of the munitions stored there.

The catastrophic explosion blew the Parthenon apart, taking off the roof and flattening three of the four walls. Later the scattered remains were used as building materials for other structures on the Acropolis, including a mosque. As a crowning insult, at the start of the nineteenth century the British Earl of Elgin claimed the authority of the sultan to remove sculptures from the site. The finest of the surviving sculptures were taken from the Acropolis and are now the pride of the British Museum in London. Other items of Parthenon statuary can be seen in other European museums, including the Louvre, despite determined Greek efforts to reclaim them.

In a roughly similar way to the Parthenon sculptures, the literature and philosophy of the Greeks survived only as lost or scattered

Religious art is one of the major contributions of Byzantine culture to the modern world. In this late Byzantine altarpiece the two central figures are subtly enhanced.

The tale of Cupid and Psyche – shown here on a Roman sarcophagus – is a Roman embellishment of a Classical Greek myth, something that occurred with increasing frequency as the two cultures merged.

texts in a score of countries, and Classical Greek culture as a whole was largely neglected in the West, even after individual texts such as the works of Aristotle and Euclid were taken up enthusiastically during the Renaissance.

Another area of Greek culture that maintained a foothold in the West was Greek mythology, which had an enduring appeal for painters and sculptors. This field also received a further stimulus during the Renaissance. Botticelli's *Birth of Venus* and *Pallas and the Centaur* are good examples of the combination of Greek myth and Renaissance humanism in the paintings of the period. Sculptors began to deliberately imitate the Greek style of art – Michelangelo's *David* being an outstanding example of the 'Classical' genre.

Even the Greek gods lurked on in a variety of disguises. For example, we find Hecate, the witch-goddess, making an appearance in Shakespeare's *Macbeth*. Perhaps the most remarkable reworking of a Greek god was the reappearance of the forest god Pan – complete with his goat's legs and horns – as the Devil himself, though he seems to have picked up a trident along the way.

The rediscovery of Greece

Thus the destruction of the Greek world contained within itself the seeds of its revival. The looting of Constantinople meant that Greek statuary and texts were carried back to western Europe, where they had the same effect as Greek artefacts and texts looted during an earlier age had had upon the Romans. That is, these embodiments of Greek culture opened the eyes of their new owners to hitherto unknown aspects of the visual arts and philosophy. The arrival soon afterwards of Greek refugees from the Ottoman occupation brought with it another wave of exposure to Greek ideas and culture.

Such exposure made members of the European elite question the status quo, and this began an intellectual ferment that combined with other nascent trends to flower into the Renaissance. However, the direct influence of Greek culture was less than the effect of Latin texts preserved by the Greeks and now transmitted to the West. The true effect of Greek culture on Western thought had to wait for the Enlightenment.

Greece itself was subjugated by the Ottoman Turks, and access to Greek sites was difficult and limited. By and large, Greece remained known to the rest of Europe only through Classical, Athenian-centric texts. Thus began the modern identification of 'ancient Greece' with Periclean Athens. This fixation largely continues to the present day, to the detriment of our understanding that Greek culture was spread far across western Europe and deep into the Middle East, both affecting and being affected by the people of these lands. Today many people are surprised to learn that the urban culture of Sicily was Greek, let alone that the Greeks founded cities near the second cataract of the Nile and in the shadow of the Himalayas.

While the rediscovery of Greek art and culture was one of the seeds that led to the flowering of the Renaissance, the Greek spirit of enquiry helped to power the spirit of the Enlightenment of the eighteenth and nineteenth centuries. This was a movement dominated by the motto *Sapere aude* – 'dare to know': a thoroughly Greek sentiment expressed in Latin.

The book that best captured the spirit of the Enlightenment was the 35-volume *Encyclopaedia* published in France and reprinted across Europe – despite the sometimes vigorous objections of the authorities. 'Encyclopaedia' itself was a portmanteau word based on what the translators fondly believed was the Greek for 'General Education' (in fact, it means something closer to 'circular learning'). The *Encyclopaedia* propagated the ideas of Aristotle and the pre-Socratic philosophers, but also brought the mechanical arts of inventors such as Heron of Alexandria to a wider audience.

Many of the ideas of the Greek philosophers were very different from those of contemporary religious authorities. Consequently, though it was intended merely as the collected body of all knowledge available at the time, the *Encyclopaedia* became one of the great subversive texts of modern history. Just as Marx's *Capital* laid the intellectual foundation of the Russian Revolution, many writers maintain that the *Encyclopaedia* prepared the ground for the French Revolution of 1789.

Other examples of the rediscovery of Greece are easily found. In 1782 France's national theatre, the Comédie Française, opened a theatre that was called the Odéon, in emulation of similar buildings that had spread across the Graeco-Roman world from the first known of such temples to the arts, the Skias of Sparta of 700 BC. There are now of course Odeons around the planet, from Vancouver to Thailand. The entertainments given there have evolved out of all recognition, but are still dramas (a Greek word) based on comedies (from the Greek *komodia*) and tragedies (*tragodia*).

During the Enlightenment architects rediscovered classical style. (As mentioned earlier, 'architecture' is also derived from the Greek word with the same meaning.) From the sixteenth to the twentieth centuries a crop of Greek-themed buildings sprang up across the Western world. One example is the Palladian neo-classical structure designed by the Irishman James Hoban in 1790. Known today as the White House, this building has housed every U.S. president of the last two hundred years. The pillar-and-architrave style of classical architecture became especially popular for banks, universities, museums and government buildings, and can be seen today on every €5 banknote.

In art the Greek myths were memorably evoked by painters such as Rubens, who produced over a dozen epic canvases with a mythological theme, and sculpture developed a 'neoclassical' school with works such as Antonio Canova's *Psyche Revived by Eros*. A knowledge of Greek literature became an essential part of an English gentleman's education. It was at a London club for such gentlemen that in 1784 a tune called 'To Anacreon in Heaven'

This Etruscan-style wine jug from Alexandria in the early Roman era is a demonstration of the Mediterranean-wide economy that was already more than a thousand years old.

The Basilica of the National Shrine of the Immaculate Conception, an example
of classic Byzantine architecture, though this building is in fact of modern
construction and located in Washington, DC.

was published. (Anacreon was a fifth-century Greek poet from the
island of Teos in the Aegean Sea. He was famous for his drinking
songs.) The words of the song are very seldom uttered these days,
but the tune has survived, fitted to a more widespread ditty called
'The Star-spangled Banner'.

It was only with the Greek War of Independence of 1821–9
that western Europe began to discover a Greece separate from the
classics. Poets such as Keats (for example, his 'Ode to a Grecian
Urn') and Byron (who was an avid Philhellene) aroused a romantic

interest that united the ideas and literature of ancient Greece with the contemporary state. Byron was famous in Britain for poems such as his lyrical 'She Walks in Beauty', but in Greece he was – and is – a national hero for his contribution to the Greek side in the war of independence fought against the Ottomans. Though Byron achieved little militarily, he highlighted the Greek cause on the world stage, and ultimately helped international recognition of Greece as an independent state (he lives on there as a leafy Athenian suburb named Byronas in his honour).

Ancient Greece in the modern era

While Europeans in the nineteenth and early twentieth century had developed a great admiration and considerable knowledge of Greek culture, there was one aspect of that culture that they abominated – homosexuality. Contemporary writers (such as E. M. Forster) had some fun with classics professors who were forced to tell students to omit parts of Classical texts that dealt with 'The Unmentionable Vice of the Greeks'. The term 'Greek love' is still sometimes used for homoeroticism, despite the despairing protests of academics that Greek homosexuality had little in common with its modern equivalent. (Indeed, anyone indulging in the most common form of 'Greek love' as practised in the Classical era would today be promptly condemned for child abuse.) However, as numerous Greek vases testified – to the horror of Victorian archaeologists – sexual relationships between adults of the same sex were not uncommon in the Classical era.

If male homosexuality was outrageous, female homosexuality was barely conceivable. The word 'lesbian' is a nineteenth-century coinage that neatly expresses both the rediscovered fascination with ancient Greece and the contemporary reaction to some of its practices. The term refers to Sappho of Lesbos, and 'Sapphist' rapidly became a euphemism for a woman sexually attracted to other women. Overall, it is clear that the modern world had – and still has – problems grappling with ancient Greek sexuality.

Sparta, for all that it was during much of its existence a dysfunctional state with severe social pathologies, has found many admirers in the modern world. No ancient state saw fit to adopt the Spartan model, and this includes the hundreds of Greek cities in the wider Greek world discussed in this text. Despite this, laconophilia (love of Sparta) has had an unhealthy influence on things as diverse as the English public school system and Prussian philosophy.

Consider this chilling statement: 'The subjugation of the helots by the Spartans was only possible because of Spartan racial superiority.' The writer of these words – Adolf Hitler – went on to argue that Germany should follow the Spartans in restricting the number of 'inferior' peoples allowed to remain alive in an ideal state.

Friedrich Nietzsche's arguments about the *übermensch* and the contrast between orderly Apollonian attitudes and the more creative Dionysian aspects of culture were perverted by the Nazis into providing moral justification for some of their more horrific acts. This happened despite the fact that such acts would have been considered equally unspeakable by the humanistic and broadly tolerant Greeks of the Seleucid and Ptolemaic kingdoms.

On the other hand, oddly enough, the most positive aspect of ancient Greece endorsed by the West probably did not originate there at all. While ancient Athens was indeed the home of an extreme democracy, this was not the first democracy in Greece (the Spartans might actually have a claim to that), nor was it the form of democracy that the West later adopted. Western democracy originated among the voting practises of the Germanic moots, though the resemblance to the Greek version certainly gave it respectability. It is also true that no modern state practices democracy in the classical Greek form. Most modern democracies are very different systems, with both a wider franchise (women can vote and there are no slaves to be excluded from doing so) and a more restricted mandate (Greek voters could vote on the issues, while modern voters get to choose someone who will vote on the issues for them).

The influence of Greek thought on modern science is everywhere apparent. Medical terms tend to be either Latin or Greek, and sound less intimidating when translated. (In Greek 'macrophage' means 'big eater', 'diarrhoea' means 'flowing through', 'haemophilia' means 'likes bleeding', and so on). Inventions of the

The Archimedes screw.

nineteenth century were often given Greek names, which is why we have, for example, the telephone ('distance talker') and photography ('light writing'). The use of such terminology is a reminder that the Greeks can lay claim to being the world's first scientists, in that they were the first people whom we know of who systematically sought out knowledge for its own sake, and developed a rigorous process of working out independently verifiable ideas from first principles.

Overall, then, the empire of Alexander may be long gone and largely forgotten, but the intellectual legacy of those who lived in that empire lives on. Not just in language, mythology and architecture or even in the free-thinking spirit of intellectual inquiry, but in that restless spirit of adventure that once propelled the ancient Greeks to new lands so far from home. The Greek legacy has become an integral part of a Western-based culture that has spread further than even the Greeks of Egypt, Iran and Afghanistan could have imagined.

In a sense, today we are all Greeks.

■✂ BIBLIOGRAPHY

Alcock, S., *Graecia Capta: The Landscapes of Roman Greece* (Cambridge, 1993)
Allen, James P., 'Language, Scripts and Literature', in *A Companion to Ancient Egypt*, ed. Alan B. Lloyd (Oxford and Malden, MA, 2010), vol. II, pp. 641–62
—, *Middle Egyptian: An Introduction to the Language and Culture of Hieroglyphs*, 3rd edn (Cambridge, 2014)
Andersen, Casper, 'The Philae Controversy: Muscular Modernization and Paternalistic Preservation', in Beth Baron, *Egypt as a Woman: Nationalism, Gender, and Politics* (Cairo, 2005)
Bar-Kochva, B., *The Seleucid Army: Organization and Tactics in the Great Campaigns* (Cambridge, 1979)
Beard, M., and J. Henderson, *Classical Art: From Greece to Rome* (Oxford, 2001)
Bilde, P., ed., *Religion and Religious Practice in the Seleucid Kingdom* (Aarhus, 1990)
Bispham, Ed, Tom Harrison and B. Sparkes, *The Edinburgh Companion to Ancient Greece and Rome* (Edinburgh, 2006)
Boardman, John, 'Aspects of "Colonization"', *Bulletin of the American Schools of Oriental Research*, CCCXXII (May 2001), pp. 33–42
Burstein, S. M., *The Hellenistic Age from the Battle of Ipsos to the Death of Kleopatra VII*, Translated Documents of Greece and Rome 3 (Cambridge, 1985)
Chaniotis, Angelos, *War in the Hellenistic World: A Social and Cultural History* (Oxford, 2005)
Crosher, Judith, *Technology in the Time of Ancient Greece* (Austin, TX, 1998)
Demand, N. H., *Urban Relocation in Archaic and Classical Greece* (London, 1990)
Eddy, S., *The King Is Dead: Studies in the Near Eastern Resistance to Hellenism, 334–31 BC* (Lincoln, NE, 1961)
Finley, M., *The World of Odysseus* (London, 1962)
Foss, Clive, and Paul Magdalino, *Rome and Byzantium: The Making of the Past* (New York, 1977)
Fowler, B. H., *Archaic Greek Poetry* (Madison, WI, and London, 1992)

Fränkel, H., *Early Greek Poetry and Philosophy* (London, 1975)

Green, Peter, *Alexander to Actium: The Historical Evolution of the Hellenistic Age* (Berkeley, CA, 1990)

Griffin, Jasper, 'The Social Function of Attic Tragedy', *Classical Quarterly*, XLVIII (1998), pp. 39–61

Hadas, Moses, 'Hellenistic Literature', *Dumbarton Oaks Papers*, XVII (1963), pp. 21, 23–35

Haldon, John, *The Empire that Would Not Die: The Paradox of Eastern Roman Survival, 640–740* (Cambridge, MA, 2016)

Hardy, D. A., ed., *Thera and the Aegean World III* (London, 1990)

Hazzard, R. A., *Imagination of a Monarchy: Studies in Ptolemaic Propaganda* (Toronto, 2000)

Holt, F. L., *Thundering Zeus: The Making of Hellenistic Bactria* (Berkeley, CA, 1999)

Hurwit, Jeffrey, *The Art and Culture of Early Greece, 1100–480 BC* (New York, 1987)

Jeffery, L. H., *Archaic Greece: The City States, c. 700–500 BC* (London, 1976)

Jenkins, Romilly J. H., 'The Hellenistic Origins of Byzantine Literature', *Dumbarton Oaks Papers*, XVII (1963), pp. 37, 39–52

Jones, A.H.M., 'The Hellenistic Age', *Past and Present*, XVII (April 1964), pp. 3–22

Kaegi, Walter, *Byzantium and the Early Islamic Conquests* (Cambridge, 1995)

Kaldellis, Anthony, *Hellenism in Byzantium: The Transformations of Greek Identity and the Reception of the Classical Tradition* (Cambridge, 2008)

Levi, Peter, *Atlas of the Greek World* (Oxford, 2000)

Lindenlauf, Astrid, 'The Sea as a Place of No Return in Ancient Greece', *World Archaeology*, XXXV/3 (2003), pp. 416–33

Maas, Michael, ed., *The Cambridge Companion to the Age of Justinian* (Cambridge, 2005)

Macurdy, G. H., *Hellenistic Queens: A Study of Woman-power in Macedonia, Seleucid, Syria, and Ptolemaic Egypt* (Baltimore, MD, 1932)

Momigliano, A., *Alien Wisdom: The Limits of Hellenization* (Cambridge, 1975)

Morris, C. D., 'The Relation of a Greek Colony to Its Mother City', *American Journal of Philology*, V/4 (1884), pp. 47–87

Neer, R., *Art and Archaeology of the Greek World: A New History, 2500 BC–150 BC* (London, 2012)

Osborne, Robin, *Classical Landscape with Figures* (London, 1987)

—, *Greece in the Making* (London, 1996)

Podlecki, A. J., *The Early Greek Poets and Their Times* (Vancouver, 1984)

Pollitt, J. J., *Art in the Hellenistic Age* (Cambridge, 1986)

Preziosi, Donald, and Louise A. Hitchcock, *Aegean Art and Architecture* (Oxford, 1999)

Rostovtzeff, Michael, 'The Hellenistic World and Its Economic Development', *American Historical Review*, XLI/2 (January 1936), pp. 231–52

—, *The Social and Economic History of the Hellenistic World*, 2nd edn (Oxford, 1951)

Samons, L., ed., *The Cambridge Companion to the Age of Pericles* (Cambridge, 2007)

Sherwin-White, S., and A. Kuhrt, *From Samarkhand to Sardis: A New Approach to the Seleucid Empire* (London, 1993)

Shipley, Graham, *The Greek World after Alexander, 323–30 BC* (London, 2000)

Silk, M. S., *Aristophanes and the Definition of Comedy* (Oxford, 2000)

Smith, R.R.R., *Hellenistic Sculpture* (London, 1991)

Snodgrass, A., *Archaic Greece: The Age of Experiment* (Berkeley, CA, 1980)

Starr, Chester G., *The Economic and Social Growth of Early Greece, 800–500 BC* (Oxford, 1977)

Strauss, Barry, *The Trojan War: A New History* (New York, 2006)

Taub, L. C., *Ptolemy's Universe* (Chicago, IL, 1993)

Thomas, R., *Herodotus in Context: Ethnography, Science, and the Art of Persuasion* (Cambridge, 2000)

Tritle, L., *The Greek World in the 4th Century: From the Fall of the Athenian Empire to the Successors of Alexander* (London, 1997)

Vermeule, Emily, *Greece in the Bronze Age* (London, 1972)

Walbank, Frank W., et al., eds, *The Cambridge Ancient History VII pt. 1: The Hellenistic World*, 2nd edn (Cambridge, 1984)

—, *The Hellenistic World*, revd edn (Cambridge, MA, 1993)

White, Mary E., 'Greek Colonization', *Journal of Economic History*, XXI/4 (December 1961), pp. 443–54

Whitmarsh, T., *Greek Literature and the Roman Empire: The Politics of Imitation* (Oxford, 2001)

PHOTO ACKNOWLEDGEMENTS

The author and publishers wish to express their thanks to the below sources of illustrative material and/or permission to reproduce it. Some locations of artworks are also given below, in the interests of brevity.

Accademia Gallery, Venice: p. 46; by or courtesy of the author: pp. 20, 25, 29, 36, 43, 67, 70, 72, 81, 97, 98, 102, 105, 110, 114, 136, 137, 149, 155 (left), 156, 163, 164, 175, 183, 190; Musée des Beaux-Arts de Brest: p. 144 (right); Biblioteca Nacional, Madrid: pp. 167, 174; British Museum, London: pp. 36, 58, 141, 144 (left); photo reproduced by permission of G. J. Faldene: p. 172; photo Maj. Mike Feeney, U.S. Army (public domain): p. 66; Guarnacci Museum, Volterra: p. 81; photograph in the Carol M. Highsmith Archive, Library of Congress, Washington, DC (Prints and Photographs Division): p. 187; J. Paul Getty Museum, Los Angeles: pp. 106, 118, 147, 159, 186; from Albert Kretchmer and Carl Rohrbach, *The Costumes of All Nations from the Earliest Times to the Nineteenth Century: Exhibiting the Dresses and Habits of all Classes* . . . (London, 1882) – photo New York Public Library: p. 169; Los Angeles County Museum of Art: pp. 21, 38, 54, 128, 179; Metropolitan Museum of Art: pp. 18, 22, 26, 30, 35, 50, 62, 74, 79, 89, 102; National Archaeological Museum, Naples: p. 51; National Gallery, London: p. 29; National Roman Museum, Rome: pp. 105, 140; photos Marie-Lan Nguyen: pp. 45, 62, 160; Ny Carlsberg Glyptotek, Copenhagen: pp. 45, 136; photo reproduced with permission from Nigel Pollard: p. 129; Sanssouci, Potsdam: p. 152; from Hermann Thiersch, *Pharos antike Islam und Occident: ein Beitrage zur Architekturgeschichte* (Leipzig and Berlin, 1909): p. 117; Vatican Museum: pp. 72, 97; Walters Art Museum, Baltimore: pp. 54, 182; photo Jackie Whalen: p. 124.

Page numbers in *italics* refer to illustrations